PREPARING
YOUR MANUSCRIPT

PREPARING YOUR MANUSCRIPT

New Revised Edition

by Elizabeth Preston

✍ ✍ ✍

Boston AUSTIN, WRITER, INC. • *Publishers*

Copyright © 1994
by
THE WRITER, INC.

First edition (1986) by Elizabeth Preston, Ingrid Monke, and Elizabeth Bickford

Library of Congress Cataloging-in-Publication Data

Preston, Elizabeth, 1950-
    Preparing your manuscript / by Elizabeth Preston. -- Rev. ed.
      p. cm.
    Includes bibliographical references and index.
    ISBN 0-87116-172-9 (pbk.) : $12.00
    1. Manuscript preparation (Authorship) 2. English language-
    -Rhetoric. I. Title.
    PN160.P74 1994   93-43417
    808'.027--dc20   CIP

PRINTED IN THE UNITED STATES OF AMERICA

CONTENTS

Preface

You have finished writing your novel, short story, article, poem, play, or nonfiction book, and your first inclination is to send it off to a publisher or editor or agent as quickly as possible. You have thought through and worked through your ideas and put them down on paper, and with a sense of relief and accomplishment, you think the manuscript is ready for submission. All too often, however, such is not the case: Your manuscript may indeed express what you want to say to the best of your ability—but have you taken into account the equally important aspect of manuscript submission? Have you made a complete, meticulous check of the *mechanics* to make sure that you are presenting it in its best light?

Manuscript preparation combines the *mechanical* as well as the *creative* side of writing: rules of grammar, correct spelling, sentence structure, word choice and usage, punctuation, composition, style, and yes, a neat well-typed manuscript. Failure to observe these rules and standards can mean rejection of your manuscript.

Preparing Your Manuscript provides a step-by-step guide to these aspects of writing for publication, so that you may — as we believe you should — check the mechanical elements in your manuscript *before* you submit it. Although it does not endeavor to be a comprehensive book on any of these topics, it covers in easy, accessible form the basics of grammar and language, punctuation, capitalization, and includes a list of words most frequently misspelled or misused. Further, you will find essentials on the procedure of submitting and marketing your work, answers to questions on copyright law as it applies to writers, and detailed information on preparing footnotes and bibliographies if you are writing a nonfiction book or research article.

Formats for playscripts, poetry, and television scripts as well as straight prose are also included, because whether you work on a typewriter, word processor, or personal computer, typing is, of course, of major importance. A sloppily typed manuscript will certainly detract from the impression your manuscript makes on an editor or publisher. To round out this valuable book, there is a selected list of widely used and respected reference books, several of which you may wish to add to your personal library.

It is our hope that *Preparing Your Manuscript* will serve as a companion to other standard books on creative writing, along with a good dictionary and thesaurus, and that using it diligently will markedly increase your chances of having your manuscripts accepted for publication.

PREPARING
YOUR MANUSCRIPT

1 Grammar and Usage

Your manuscript should be as grammatically correct and as smooth in construction as possible. Experienced writers know that good composition, with the right word in the right place, and attention to rules of grammar are necessary factors in any type of writing. Although there may be some successful writers who occasionally disregard conventional usage, generally speaking, the reputation of such writers has to be outstanding for them to be able to do this. In any case, the beginning writer should certainly be aware of common errors and know how to avoid making them.

Entire books are available on the details and variations in grammar and usage; for the purpose of this handbook, we'll cover the most important points of this large subject. These include common errors in grammar; proper placement of phrases and clauses; and the words most often used incorrectly, with illustrations of correct usage.

Grammar

A complete sentence is made up of two main parts: The subject (noun or pronoun, plus adjectives and articles—the, a, an) and the predicate (a verb plus adverbs that may modify it).

A clause consists of a subject and a predicate (i.e., it is a sentence in construction), but is itself part of, and has a definite function in, a longer sentence. Clauses are classified as follows:

Main—the sentence itself in its simple form; the clause on which the rest of the sentence depends. (Jane sent her manuscript to Houghton Mifflin.)

Subordinate—depends on the main clause; cannot stand on its own, as the main clause can. (Jane sent her story to Houghton Mifflin, *where she had a friend in the editorial department.*)

Coordinate—a clause of the same rank as another, coordinate with a main clause or with a subordinate clause. Coordinate clauses are connected by coordinating conjunctions—and, but, or. (Jane sent her story to Houghton Mifflin, where she had a friend in the editorial department, *and she tried to be optimistic.*)

Various aspects of sentence construction can cause problems for even the most experienced writers, and these are discussed in the following section.

1. Agreement. The subject and verb must always agree in number. Do not use a singular subject with a plural verb. Such an error often occurs when one or more words separate the subject from the verb. The following examples have singular subjects:

> *One* of the boys *is working* at The Green Grocer's.

4

The *list* of magazines *includes Time* and *News-week.*

The *extent* to which VCRs are now being used in homes *is* likely to lead to great changes in the motion picture industry.

Mistakes are often made when the subject follows the verb. In the following sentences the subjects are plural:

There *are the women* who belong to the chorus.

What we seek *are an old-fashioned romance story and a suspenseful mystery.*

Where *are the museum and the planetarium?*

Another construction that takes a plural rather than a singular verb is "he is one of those men who . . ." In the sentence "He is one of those journalists who reports on The White House," the noun *one* does not govern the verb; the noun *journalist* does. The sentence should be "He is one of those *journalists* who *report* on The White House." This is clear when the sentence is turned around: "Of those *journalists* who *report* on The White House, he is one."

One of the most common misconceptions about English usage is that a noun which is not immediately perceived as plural (ending in *s* or some other clearly plural construction) must take a singular verb. But consider this sentence: "A number of hurricanes are expected this summer." You may want to assume that *number* is singular, and should, therefore, be followed by *is;* but number is really a collective noun, and it can take a singular or plural verb, depending on the sense of the sentence. A collective noun is singular if it

5

stresses the total group, but plural if the individuals making up the group are stressed. In the sentence above, it's the *hurricanes* that are expected this summer—the plural concept takes a plural verb. But in "The number of child abuse cases is appalling," it's the singular concept of *number* that is emphasized, and therefore, the verb is singular. Among the many nouns that can be considered either singular or plural are *audience, average, couple, family, variety, majority, group, number, pair, public,* and *set.*

2. Adjectives and adverbs. Adjectives modify only nouns and pronouns. Adverbs may modify verbs, adjectives, and other adverbs. Do not use an adjective in place of an adverb, or vice versa. "He always *drives* very *careful* in traffic" is incorrect. The word *careful* is an adjective, and should not be used to modify or describe the verb *drives.* You should use an adverb: "He always *drives* very *carefully* in traffic." Or, if you wish to use an adjective, recast the sentence: "He is a very *careful driver* in traffic."

When forms of the verb to be and verbs pertaining to the senses (feel, smell, taste, etc.) make up the predicate, the modifier following the verb is an adjective, called a predicate adjective. It is incorrect to say "It smells *badly*," "The cake *tastes deliciously*," because *badly* and *deliciously* are adverbs. Here are the corrected sentences: "It *smells bad.*" "The cake *tastes delicious.*"

3. Avoid shifts in person, number, or gender.
(a) In "*Everyone* was asked to state *their* opinion," there is a shift in number. *Everyone* is singular; *their* is

plural. Reworded correctly the sentence reads: "*Everyone* was asked to state *his or her* opinion."

(b) The following illustrates a shift in person: "*Anyone* who forgot to do his homework is going to be sorry *you* came to class today." This sentence is wrong because *anyone* and *you* do not agree in person: *Anyone* is third person, *you* is second person. This sentence can be recast as "*Anyone* who forgot to do *his* homework is going to be sorry *he* came to class today." A shift in person often occurs in a series of sentences: "*No one* is to forget to do *his* homework. *You'll* be sorry if *you* do—especially if the teacher gives *us* a test."

(c) The following illustrates a shift in gender: "The cat ate *her* dinner before *it* ran away." This is wrong because the gender changes from female *(her)* to neuter *(it)*. You may say: "The cat ate *her* dinner before *she* ran away." Or, if you wish, "The cat ate *its* dinner before *it* ran away." Gender must be consistent.

4. Case of nouns and pronouns. The case of a noun or pronoun is determined by the function of the word within the sentence. It may be the subject of a verb (*I* am the queen), the object of a verb or preposition (He gave it to *me*), or the possessive modifier of another word (That is *my* hat). *I, me,* and *my* are called the nominative, objective, and possessive forms. Other forms are *you/you/your, he/him/his, she/her/her, we/us/our,* and *they/them/their.* Some of the trickiest points regarding case are as follows:

(a) Errors after the verb *to be:* Although "That's him" is frequently heard in conversation, "That is he" is the correct form. Of course, there's a great difference between writing prose and writing dialogue for fiction; in conversation or dialogue, you'll probably use the casual "It's me" more frequently than "It is I." It would be a revealing characteristic to have a character say, "These are they" or "It is I," since formal language is not often heard in everyday conversation.

(b) Errors with *as* and *than* are often made because the second verb is dropped from the sentence: "He is older *than* me" is correctly written "He is older *than* I [am]." "Terry is *as* enthusiastic *as* him" should be "Terry is *as* enthusiastic *as* he [is]."

(c) Errors with *between*. *Between* is always followed by pronouns in the objective case. "*Between* you and me" is the proper phrase.

(d) Errors with *who/whoever* and *whom/whomever*. *Who* and *whoever* are the nominative forms used whenever the pronoun functions as the subject: "*Who* wrote the book?" "*Whoever* wakes up first makes the coffee." *Whom* and *whomever,* the objective forms, are employed when the pronoun is the object of the verb or preposition: "*Whom* do you want to thank?" Problems arise because the pronoun is sometimes mistakenly identified as the object of the verb when it is really the subject of the clause, as in the following:

> I want to thank the man *who* wrote the book.

> I want to thank *whoever* wrote the book. (*Whoever* is the subject of the clause *whoever wrote the book.*)

Sometimes a phrase such as *I think* or *I believe* will interrupt a "who" clause, but this doesn't affect the clause:

> I want to thank *whoever you think wrote* the book.

8

Errors are often made after the preposition *between*. In "This is a contest *between whoever won the relay and Harry Wilson*," *whoever* is the subject of the clause *whoever won the relay;* be sure not to use the objective *whomever* in this case.

(e) Errors with compound objects.

"Jim took *Sally and me* to the seashore" is correct, but it very often written incorrectly as "Jim took *Sally and I* to the seashore"—probably as a result of the mistaken notion that *Sally and I* sounds better than *Sally and me. Sally and me* is the object of the verb (took). If you drop *Sally* from the sentence, the error is obvious: You wouldn't say, "Jim took *I* to the seashore." The use of the pronoun *myself* instead of *me* as part of a compound object—"He took *Susan and myself* to the seashore"—is *not* acceptable, either.

Sentence structure

In the foregoing examples and illustrations, we have concentrated on grammar. It is equally important for you to consider sentence structure. A poorly constructed sentence may be clumsy and confusing. Here are some useful suggestions:

1. All parts of a sentence that are parallel in meaning should be parallel in structure.

(a) Use conjunctions carefully. Do not join unparallel ideas or words with *and* or *or*.

> Did he advise him *to enlist* in the army now *or that he should* wait for two years? (Wrong)

> Did he advise him *to enlist* in the army now *or to wait* for two years? (Right)

(b) Correlative conjunctions—*either . . . or/neither*

. . . nor/ not only . . . but (also)—join complementary words, phrases, and clauses. These conjunctions are frequently mismatched or misplaced in a sentence. Make sure that each of the two correlatives is followed by the same part of speech.

> The writer selected *either the red pen or* used *the blue one.* (Wrong)

> The writer selected *either the red pen or the blue one.* (Right)

> *Neither he nor his colleague* selected the red pen. (Right)

> *Not only* did the *jewel thief* murder her husband *but also the butler.* (Wrong)

> The jewel thief murdered *not only her husband but also the butler.* (Right)

(c) All items in a series must be parallel:

> His responsibilities included *filing* the statements, *cashing* the checks, and *the operation* of the Teletype machine. (Wrong)

> His responsibilities included *filing* the statements, *cashing* the checks, and *operating* the Teletype machine. (Right)

> The jaguar is *swift, quiet,* and *moves with grace.* (Wrong)

> The jaguar is *swift, quiet,* and *graceful.* (Right)

2. Misplaced modifiers. The position of a modifier affects the meaning of a sentence. Be sure to place the modifier so that it modifies the correct word or phrase.

(a) Note how the meaning changes in each of the following examples:

Only I sold three bracelets.

I *only* sold three bracelets.

I sold *only* three bracelets.

I ran *almost* three miles.

I *almost* ran three miles.

(b) A phrase or a clause misplaced in a sentence may seem to modify a word or a phrase that it doesn't logically modify:

I am enclosing proof that I have given birth to only two children in this envelope.

Better: I am enclosing in this envelope proof that I have given birth to only two children.

She is taking a workshop on how to make a kimono from a Japanese nun.

Better: She is taking a workshop from a Japanese nun on how to make a kimono.

The assailant was described as a five-foot-nine-inch man, with a heavy moustache weighing 155 to 160 pounds.

Better: The assailant was described as a five-foot-nine-inch man weighing 155 to 160 pounds, with a heavy moustache.

(c) Dangling participle. A participial phrase (wringing her hands, swinging his arms, etc.) at the beginning of a clause must modify the subject of the clause. A misplaced participle can modify the wrong noun or pronoun and produce an absurd sentence:

Having rotted in the damp cellar, *she* was unable to sell the apples.

Better: Having rotted in the damp cellar, *the apples* could not be sold.

11

Or recast the sentence: She was unable to sell the apples, which had rotted in the damp cellar.

Turning the corner, *the magnificent sunset* came into view.

Better: Turning the corner, *I saw* the magnificent sunset.

3. Be careful in the use of pronouns. Whenever a pronoun is used in place of a noun or pronoun, the word it replaces, its antecedent, must be understood.

Battles between the American Indians and white men came about in part because *they* oppressed *them*. (It is not clear whether "they" refers to Indians or white men. It is also difficult to know what "them" refers to.)

Avoid overusing pronouns:

Tom said *it* was a good game, but said *it* seemed to him *it* might have had more action in the last part of *it*.

Commonly Misused Words

Accept and *except*. To *accept* anything means to take or receive it. To *except* something means to omit or exclude it. Here are examples of the correct use of these words:

Did you *accept* Mary's invitation to the party?

I hope you will *accept* this small gift.

She liked all the dresses *except* the gray one.

Everyone *except* Henry arrived on time.

Advise and *inform*. *Advise* means to give advice or counsel. *Inform* means to tell or give information. These words are used correctly in the following:

The lawyer will *advise* his client what procedure is necessary.

Did you *advise* her to go to the doctor?

The letter was to *inform* me that he would visit New York.

He will *inform* us when the bill is due.

Affect and *effect*. *Affect*, a verb, means to impress or influence; also, to imitate, feign. *Effect*, as a verb, means to bring to pass, to accomplish:

How did the music *affect* you?

The rain may *affect* the golf tournament.

She was deeply *affected* by the death of her friend.

She *affected* an English accent.

Congress will try to *effect* changes in the budget this year.

As a noun, *effect* means immediate result, consequence.

What was the *effect* of his accident on his career?

The new law will have a profound *effect* on our lives.

In the plural form it means goods or possessions:

There were some valuable antiques among his *effects*.

All ready and *already*. *All ready* (two words), meaning completely prepared, is used adjectively, as in: "We are *all ready* for the party." *Already* (one word) is an adverb expressing time. It means by this time, before, previously, as in: "She had *already* left when I telephoned."

All right (two words) can be used correctly only in the following way: "It is *all right* for you to take your vacation next week." *Alright* (one word) is not acceptable usage.

All together and *altogether*. *All together* means in a group, as in "We ate dinner *all together*." *Altogether* means entirely or completely, as in "He had *altogether* misunderstood me" or "There were six ball players *altogether*."

Alternate and *alternative*. *Alternate*, as an adjective, means occurring by successive turns (it has another meaning as a verb); *alternative*, usually used as a noun, indicates a choice between two possibilities. "John and Mary serve on *alternate* days." "War was our only *alternative*."

Appraise and *apprise*. Do not use *appraise*, meaning to evaluate, when you mean *apprise*, to inform, as in "She was *apprised* (informed) of the situation." *Appraise* is properly used in "The dealer is coming to *appraise* the quality and value of the Oriental rugs."

As and *like*. These two words are increasingly used incorrectly, though the rules governing their usage are fairly straightforward. *Like* is a preposition used in phrases to compare nouns and pronouns. Here are examples of correct usage: "Jeanne looks *like* her mother." "Eric acts *like* a child." "The car runs *like* a top." Since prepositions take an object, the noun or pronouns following *like* must be in the objective case: *like* her and me, not *like* she and I. *As* is a conjunction introducing clauses of comparison, which, like all

14

clauses, must contain a verb. The following sentence is wrong: "I wish I could cook *like* she does." It should read, "I wish I could cook *as* (the way) she does." Another example of correct usage: "We don't get along *as* good friends should." The general rule of thumb is to use *as* if a verb follows the noun or pronoun; use *like* if there is no verb.

Beside and *besides*. *Beside,* meaning next to, should not be confused with *besides,* meaning in addition to.

> Tim's book was *beside* his bed.
>
> There were several books *besides* these in his room.

Between and *among*. Remember that *between* is generally used in speaking of only *two* persons or things; *among* is used in speaking of more than two. Here are examples of correct usage:

> The jewelry was divided *between* Eleanor and Mary.
>
> There were only two novels *among* the ten books.
>
> She had a choice *between* candy and flowers.

Capital and *capitol*. A *capitol* is a building—the State *capitol*. *Capital* has several meanings:

> Begin the sentence with a *capital* letter.
>
> What is the *capital* of Wyoming?
>
> That's a *capital* idea!
>
> He didn't have enough *capital* to finance the construction.

Compare to and *compare with*. Use *compare with* for comparison of similarities and differences: "Darlene *compared* her homework answers *with* those of her classmates." Use *compare to* for analogy: "Sam *compared* his father-in-law *to* Scrooge."

Cite and *site*. *Cite* is a verb meaning to identify or to list: "He *cited* five reasons for our involvement in South Africa." *Site* is a noun meaning location. "That will be the perfect *site* for our mobile home."

Complement and *compliment*. *Complement* may be used as a verb or a noun. It refers to something that enhances or completes: "The blue scarf *complements* her dress." *Compliment*, a noun or a verb, expresses approval or praise: "He *complimented* her on her good taste."

Different from and *different than*. *Different from* is preferred—Chopin's music is *different from* Beethoven's—although you can use *than* with *different* when it is followed by a clause: "The way women dress today is *different than* it was a century ago."

Discreet and *discrete*. *Discreet* means careful or modest: "He acknowledged her presence with a *discreet* nod." *Discrete* means separate, distinct, as in "The book is organized in *discrete* units."

Disinterested and *uninterested*. *Disinterested* means impartial and unbiased; *uninterested* indicates indifference: "A judge is *disinterested* in the cases before him—not *uninterested*."

Due to. This term is frequently misused, as in the following sentence: "*Due to* the storm, school was cancelled." Here, due is used wrongly as a preposition, when in fact it is an adjective, and therefore must modify a noun or pronoun. The best place for *due to* is after a form of the verb to be, because there it will

16

always serve as an adjective. Corrected, the above sentence reads, "School cancellation was *due to* the storm" (*due* modifies cancellation). If proper placement of *due to* in a sentence still confuses you, try replacing it with *caused by* or *attributed to;* if the replacement makes sense, *due to* is correctly used, as in "Her mood swings are *due to (caused by)* the medication she's taking."

Each other and *one another*. *Each other* has to do with two persons. *One another* has to do with more than two.

The two boys resemble *each other*.

The four boys resemble *one another*.

Fewer and *less*. Use *fewer* for comparing specific numbers: "There are *fewer* than ten students in the class." *Less* is used with a quantity or mass: "There is *less* noise in the country." "There is *less* oil available now than ten years ago."

Good and *well*. *Good* is an adjective; *well* is used primarily as an adverb. *Good* is commonly used incorrectly in such sentences as: "The child is walking *good*." "He plays his trumpet *good*." Corrected, we have: "The child is walking *well*." "He plays his trumpet *well*."

Hanged and *hung*. Things are *hung* when they are suspended. People are *hanged* when they are executed.

Imply and *infer*. *Imply* means to suggest or hint: "She *implied* that I was unstable." *Infer* means to deduce, draw a conclusion: "Reading my medical records led her to *infer* that I was unstable."

Ingenious and *ingenuous*. There's a difference of just one letter in these two words, but such a difference in meaning! An *ingenious* person is a clever or skillful one. An *ingenuous* person is one who is frank and artless, naïve.

Insure and *assure*. Both *insure* and *assure* mean to protect or make safe, but only *assure* can be used in regard to people, in the sense of setting someone's mind at rest. "He *assured* the general that the enemy would not attack." *Insure* also means to protect from harm or loss, as in "You must *insure* your house." *Ensure* is a variant of *insure*.

Irregardless and *regardless*. *Irregardless* is heard frequently, but it's not acceptable, standard usage. The proper word is *regardless*.

Its and *it's*. *Its* is the possessive form of it: "The cat licked *its* paw." *It's* is the contraction of *it is* or *it has:* "*It's* a beautiful day!" "*It's* been so long!"

Kind of and *sort of*. These expressions mean *a type of*—not rather or somewhat. "I'm *kind of* glad I finished my exam" should not be used. "This is *the kind of* novel she writes" is correct. Make sure you do not mix singular and plural words when using these expressions: "What *sorts of books* are in stock?" "Does she knit *this kind of sweater?*"

Lay and *lie*. We *lay* (meaning put) an object down. We *lie* down (to rest). A hen *lays* an egg. A book *lies* on the table. *Lay* means to place an object on a table or floor; *lie* means to recline or rest.

Confusion arises from the fact that the past tense of *lie* is *lay* and similar to *lay* (put) in the present tense:

> I *lie* down for an hour. (Present)
>
> I *lay* down for an hour. (Past)

18

He *lays* the book down. (Present)

He *laid* the book down. (Past)

Lend and *loan*. In accepted, conventional usage, *lend* is a verb; *loan* is a noun. "I *lend* him money." "He asked for a *loan*." However, *loan* is now often used and accepted as a verb: "He *loaned* her five dollars."

May and *can*. *May* should be used for asking permission: "*May* I give you a ride home?" Or possibility: "We *may* be able to reach New York by morning." *Can* implies ability to do, either physical or mental: "How *can* she accomplish so much in one week?" "I *can* think of no reason why Elliot embezzled the money."

Principal and *principle*. *Principal* may be used as either a noun or an adjective: "Peter was sent to the *principal* (head) of the school for his misbehavior." "Do you know the *principal* (main) products of Venezuela?" "The chairman hopes to increase the *principal* (capital) of the firm by his new investments." *Principle* is always used as a noun, never as an adjective: "What is the underlying *principle* (essential element) of Plato's philosophy?"

Precede and *proceed*. *Precede* means to go ahead or in front of: "One man can *precede* his friend in boarding a train." *Proceed* means to move forward: "He must *proceed* with the presentation of his case." "I will *proceed* with the writing of my novel."

Set and *sit*. *Set* means to place; *sit* means to take a position. "He *set* the plates on the table." "I'll *sit* at the table."

Stationary and *stationery*. Another pair of words spelled the same except for one letter, but entirely different in meaning. *Stationery*—paper, pencils, pens, etc.—is sold by a stationer. *Stationary* means fixed in a certain station or position—not moving or changing place, as, a *stationary* engine.

That and *which*. These relative pronouns are two of the most often misused words in the English language. *That* is used only for restrictive clauses—clauses essential to the sense of a sentence; *which* is used for non-restrictive, parenthetical clauses—clauses that are not essential to the sense of a sentence (but modify or expand the meaning). For instance, "There's the car *that* I want to buy" would make no sense without the phrase "*that* I want to buy." On the other hand, "The old courthouse, *which* was built in 1712, is in the middle of town" would still make sense if the "which" clause were omitted. Also, "which" clauses are set off by commas; "that" clauses are not.

Try. *Try* must be followed by an infinitive—not *and*. "*Try* and tell me what to do!" is incorrect. It should be: "*Try to* tell me what to do!"

Was and *were*. In certain subjunctive constructions, *were* is used instead of *was* with I, he, and she. Use the subjunctive in statements contrary to fact: "I wish I *were* a millionaire." The subjunctive is often necessary in clauses beginning with "if": "She wouldn't have to wear a sweater if it *were* warmer outside." When the "if" clause is a statement of fact, the subjunctive is not necessary: "I wondered if she *was* a widow."

Where. *Where* refers to location, but is often used incorrectly to introduce a statement: "I read *where* she was going to withdraw from the race." This should be: "I read *that* she was going to withdraw from the race."

While and *though*. *While* means during the time: "*While* (during the time) Everett was taking a walk, I prepared lunch." *Though* means in spite of the fact, even if: *"Though* (in spite of the fact) Nancy couldn't afford to pay for a trip, she agreed to go anyway."

Your and *you're.* *Your* is a possessive pronoun: *your* coat, *your* hat, etc. *You're* is a contraction for *you are:* *"You're* late for work!"

2 || Punctuation

Proper punctuation—the division of a sentence or group of sentences by certain marks—is essential to making the meaning of written or printed matter clear. For instance, the addition or omission of a comma may entirely change the meaning of a sentence. Here, we'll consider those marks commonly used today in general literary works.

There are many variations of the general rules for punctuating written material, depending largely on the kind of writing you are doing. The following rules are generally acceptable to all publishers and printers.

PERIOD (.)

A period is used as follows:

1. At the end of a declarative sentence:

> Experimental and literary fiction will be considered.

2. After an imperative sentence *not* requiring an exclamation point:

Be sure to send in any poems you have written in the past year.

3. After a rhetorical question that does not require a question mark:

The question is whether we can find a replacement in time.

4. After an indirect question:

He asked whether his manuscript had been received.

5. After abbreviations: *Ms., Mr., Mrs., Dr., Prof.,* etc.

6. After initials:

R. D. Preston   Ellen M. Webster

7. As a decimal point:

26.42 per cent $3.50 a pair

8. With parentheses, the period is placed inside the parentheses if the parenthetical material is a complete sentence:

He wouldn't let anyone read the poems he had written. (I don't know if anyone can change his mind.)

Place the period outside the parentheses when the parenthetical expression is an integral part of the sentence:

Mark would not take his editor's advice (even though he knew the criticism was justified).

Omit the period at the end of a complete parenthetical sentence when it interrupts the main sentence:

> Eleanor finally sent her manuscript to the publisher (she had kept it in her desk for a month), which took a great deal of persuasion.

If the parenthetical element (even though it is in itself a complete sentence) comes at the end of the main sentence, place the period outside the final parenthesis:

> I finally persuaded Janet to submit her novel (this took a monumental effort).

9. The period is always placed inside quotation marks.

> "I'll be ready as soon as I type this paragraph."

EXCLAMATION POINT (!)

The exclamation point is properly used after words, phrases, or sentences expressing strong emotion or surprise.

> What a wonderful person our chairman is!
>
> Oh, no! You couldn't do that to me!
>
> Great! Wonderful! Better than we could hope for!

The exclamation point is placed inside quotation marks if it is part of the quoted material.

> "Good work!" the coach shouted.

Never use double punctuation at the end of sentences or questions (i.e., both inside and outside of quotation marks and parentheses).

QUESTION MARK (?)

A question mark is used:
1. After every direct question.

> What is the name of the book you're reading?

A question mark is *not* used after an indirect question.

> She asked her neighbors where they had lived previously.

2. For more than one question in the same sentence.

> Do you write short stories? Poems? Articles?

The question mark is placed inside quotation marks if the question is part of the quoted material.

> "Where did you put my book?" she asked.

But

> Who called "Traitor! Traitor!" when he passed?

3. After an implied question in a declarative sentence.

> You mean you don't find this book exciting?

QUOTATION MARKS
DOUBLE (" ") AND SINGLE (' ')

Double quotation marks are used:
1. To enclose a direct quotation.

> "This is the proper form to use," said the teacher.

2. To enclose a word or words used as slang or as a nickname.

Al Smith, "The Happy Warrior"

"Foggy Bottom," The Old State Department

Thomas P. "Tip" O'Neill

The geyser at Yellowstone Park ("Old Faithful") is an awesome sight.

3. To set off titles of stories, articles, poems, or parts of long works, and television shows.

Did you know that Cynthia's story, "Bereft," was included in the new collection?

The "Punctuation" section of this book is very long.

The article, "Collecting Autographs," has just been published.

"Nightline" is my favorite show.

Titles of books, newspapers and magazines are usually printed in italics (indicated by underlining in typewritten copy), as are titles of motion pictures and stage plays.

I've been trying to find out whether Mike's article appeared in *The Mother Earth News*.

Jack Nicholson starred in *The Shining*.

Cats is a fabulous show for all ages.

A quotation within a quotation is enclosed in single quotation marks.

Grace said, "Lisa left after remarking bitterly, 'It isn't everyone who would do so much for a friend.'"

Of course Grace was angry, and when she left the room she said, "I can't forget Kate's remark. I don't know how she could say, 'You don't think of anyone but yourself.' "

Quotation marks are always placed outside the period and comma; either outside or inside such punctuation marks as the question mark, exclamation point, or parentheses, unless such punctuation marks belong with the quoted material.

The following sentences show various uses of quotation marks in combination with other points of punctuation.

"Evelyn," the doctor said, "will be ready to leave the hospital at any time."

Fred continued his story: "It began to rain just before we left for camp. George was—" he hesitated, "well—he didn't seem at all happy with the plan."

"Will Maggie go on the trip with us?" I asked.

Can anyone tell me the origin of the expression "as good as gold"?

Ellen stared at him and said, "So, he's the famous 'Boston Brahmin'."

"I like your story," she commented, "the one that begins 'Prisons are not always places with bars—,' and then continues about the prisons we make for ourselves."

Tom looked very worried as he said, "It will be a case for experts"; then, abruptly, "but you are an expert, I suppose," he said, smiling at Jennie.

"Watch your step! Careful!" Peter cautioned.

Do not use quotation marks to enclose an indirect quotation.

Janet said "that the work should have been done the day before." (Wrong)

Janet said that the work was already finished. (Right)

COMMA (,)

A comma is used:

1. To separate words, phrases, clauses, letters, and figures in a series. Although a comma may be used to separate the last two units in a series, it is not necessary.

> Lawyers, doctors, and architects occupy most of the offices in this building.
>
> The vowels a, e, i, o, u appear more frequently than the letters x, y, and z.
>
> The first three stops on the trip will be New York, Baltimore and Washington.
>
> Congress discussed the farm bill, the budget and social security.

2. To set off an adverbial clause or introductory phrase at the beginning of a sentence, or words like *too* (meaning *also*) within or at the end of a sentence:

> When the audience finally settled down, the speaker began his lecture.
>
> Knowing that Jill was in town, I decided to invite her for dinner.
>
> The doctor, too, thought the woman needed a special nurse.
>
> My attorney wanted to bring suit, too.

3. To separate two adjectives modifying the same word:

She is an intelligent, lively woman.

A comma should not be used to separate such adjectives if one adjective is closely connected in thought with the word modified.

> She wore her heavy, brown coat. (Wrong)
> She wore her heavy brown coat. (Right)

4. To separate identical words.

> If the work is left to Mary, Mary will do it well.

The only exception to this rule is illustrated by the following sentence:

> He told me that that was the correct answer.

5. To set off direct quotations.

> "I am going," he said, taking up his cane.

6. To set off *yes* and *no*.

> Yes, you may submit your proposal.

7. Before a title that follows a proper name.

> Suzanne Hill, D.D.S.   Henry Dawson, Ph.D.

8. Between the name of a person and the name of an organization.

> Vice-President, Women's City Club

9. When the natural order of a sentence is inverted.

> When he shuts the door with a bang, look out!

10. Between the city and the state.

> Boston, MA 02116

11. After *i.e., viz., as, that is,* etc.

Did he tell you where he would stay; that is, at what hotel?

12. Before a conjunction that joins coordinate clauses.

I go to work at eight o'clock, but Maud does not go until nine.

13. Between words or phrases repeated to give emphasis.

I will go, I will, I will, I will!

14. Commas are used in pairs:
(a) To enclose a word or words used appositively.

Mr. Jones, the clerk, comes at nine o'clock.

Henry, the security guard, just left the building.

(b) To enclose a word, phrase, or clause used parenthetically.

You will, of course, need a heavy coat.

There is, however, a more important matter to consider.

When the word *however* is used as a modifier, it should not be enclosed by commas.

I noticed that *however* slowly the ferry appeared to be moving, it never took more than a few minutes to reach the opposite shore.

(c) To enclose an expression used in direct address.

And are you, Mr. Jenks, going with us?

Sometimes in dialogue, to give the sentence as it sounds, the first comma is omitted.

Well sir, how long will you be here?

O my friends, how I have missed you!

(d) To enclose the year in the date when used within a sentence.

He came to work for our company on March 2, 1972, and is still with us.

Commas are not used when only the month and year are given.

It was in May 1981 that we went to Europe.

Never separate a subject from its verb with a comma.

Any piece of work that has to be done carefully, should never be done in haste. (Wrong)

Any piece of work that has to be done carefully should never be done in haste. (Right)

A comma should not be used between an adjective and the noun it modifies.

The man is an efficient, worker. (Wrong)

The man is an efficient worker. (Right)

A comma should not be used with a dash.

Do you know that woman,—the one in blue? (Wrong)

Do you know that woman—the one in blue? (Right)

A comma is always placed inside quotation marks.

"I know the place," he said.

COLON (:)

A colon is used:

1. To introduce a formal quotation or a direct question.

> Professor Evans began to speak: "This is a gathering of the most important writers in the area."

> This is the question before us: Will writers benefit from joining an authors workshop?

2. After the salutation of a formal letter.

> Dear Mr. Montgomery: Gentlemen:

A comma is sometimes used after the salutation in an informal letter:

> Dear Henry Talbot,   Dear Jenny,

3. Before a series:

> Here are some interesting titles: *All the Way Home, An Island in the Sun, Who's Afraid of Virginia Woolf?, None of the Above.*

4. After *the following, as follows, in the following order, thus,* etc.:

> An itinerary will include the following cities: New York, Chicago, St. Louis, Dallas, and Los Angeles.

5. Between two independent clauses, the second of which supplements the first.

> He followed the instructions to the letter: the work was finished late that evening.

6. In bibliographical listings, between place of publication and the name of the publisher:

> Kenison, Katrina, Ed. *The Best American Short Stories 1993*. Boston: Houghton Mifflin Company, 1993.

7. To separate the numbers of a chapter and verse in a Biblical reference.

> I Corinthians 15: 20-22
>
> John 8:51

8. Between hour and minutes when indicating the time of day.

> 7:15 A.M.   3:30 P.M.

9. Before a detailed list.

> These are the things you must do today: return your books to the library; mail the package; and, finally, pick up your suit at the cleaners.

The colon is placed outside quotation marks, unless it is part of the material being quoted.

SEMICOLON (;)

A semicolon indicates a break in thought that is greater than that indicated by the comma, but less than that shown by the colon or period.

Here are some of its uses:

1. Between main clauses not joined by a conjunction *(and, or, but,* etc.).

> I had planned to continue writing through the afternoon; as it happened, unexpected guests arrived.

2. To separate clauses or a series of sentences in which commas are used.

> Every day, including Sundays and holidays, he took his walk; his wife, however, sat on the porch rocking and knitting; and their teenage son, always restless, threw the basketball against the garage door.

3. When *for instance, namely,* or *for example* precede a long series.

> He never sat down to write without making certain preparations; for example, he put his dictionary next to him; sharpened several pencils; and put a stack of paper on the table next to his desk.

4. To complete short sentences that are related but independent.

> The brothers were not at all alike in their tastes: Evan liked basketball; George was a reader; John sat for hours working with his computer.

In general, a semicolon is used where the meaning might not be clear by the use of commas alone.

The semicolon should be placed outside quotation marks (unless it is part of the matter being quoted) and following the closing parentheses.

DASH (—)

In typewritten copy, a dash is usually indicated by two hyphens with no spacing in between.

A dash is used:

1. To indicate a sudden break in a sentence, a

change in thought, hesitancy, or to set off an expression used parenthetically.

> "I want so much to—" George could not go on.

> I can't leave home even for a—Here is my father now.

> He's not exactly irresponsible—but—well, you've seen how he acts.

2. For emphasis of an expressed idea or phrase.

> I beg you—What more can I do?—come to see my brother.

3. To summarize a statement.

> Jones, Astor, and Ellison—all three were gone.

4. To indicate omission of parts of words or phrases.

> Janet R— won't let herself be quoted.

> In the last—no one came.

5. A short dash (typed as a single hyphen) is used between page numbers, dates, and the like.

> 1980–83   pp. 46–49

A dash is often used before the name of an author or source of a quotation.

> "And wind came up out of the sea,
> And said, 'O mists, make room for me.'"
> —Longfellow

A dash is placed inside quotation marks if it is part of the quoted matter; otherwise; outside.

> "Why don't you go into town or—?"

But

He asked Joe, "Why don't you go into the office?"—but he immediately knew that was a mistake.

APOSTROPHE (')

An apostrophe is used:
1. To indicate the possessive case.

> The man's heavy suitcase weighed him down.
>
> The lawyers' cases were becoming more complex every year.
>
> The women's coats were moved to the third floor.
>
> Her son-in-law's behavior puzzled her.

In conventional usage, the possessive singular of proper names ending in *s*, *x*, or *z* is formed by adding an apostrophe and an *s*.

> The Roberts's house is really a mansion.

Current usage often adds only an apostrophe to form the singular possessive after words or names ending in *s*, *x*, *z*, or when the addition of an *s* makes the word or name awkward or difficult to pronounce.

> The Evans' shoe store is in my building.

2. To form the plural of letters, numbers, and abbreviations with periods.

> You can see that e's and r's are very common in the English language.
>
> All odd numbers were used: 5's, 7's and 9's.
>
> The University awarded twenty M.A.'s and Ph.D.'s in the chemistry department last year.

However, the apostrophe is often omitted in writing these plurals, especially in dates: *1870s* for *1870's*. Either is correct.

3. To mark the omission of part of a date.

the class of '86
The Hurricane of '38

4. To indicate the omission of letters in contractions, dialect, or colloquial speech.

She's [for *she is*] getting very nervous.

We don't [for *do not*] like their life style.

They wouldn't [for *would not*] contribute to our fund.

Do not use an apostrophe in a possessive pronoun.

He chose the painting because of *it's* bright colors. (Wrong)

He chose the painting because of its bright colors. (Right)

Sometimes the apostrophe is used though possession is not indicated, especially with expressions of duration.

He did a good day's work.

There was a month's delay in production.

On the other hand, the apostrophe is often (but not necessarily) omitted when no possession is meant.

He attended three writers conferences this summer.
[Writers' conferences may also be used.]

The publishers meetings went very well today.
[or publishers' meeting]

PARENTHESES ( )

Parentheses are used:

1. To enclose a word, phrase, or a complete sentence that explains, clarifies, or expands on a statement when the general meaning of the words or main sentence does not depend on the parenthentical material (and may be read without it).

> The rent control laws (adopted in 1984) were not clearly understood by the city's property owners.

2. To enclose a figure inserted after a written number

> The total number of boxes in the shipment is forty-thousand (40,000).

> The contract calls for a payment of ninety-five ($95.00) dollars a month.

3. To enclose figures or letters indicating items in a series or divisions of a subject.

> For camp you will need to bring: (a) two blankets; (b) four sheets; (c) two pillowcases; and (d) one pillow.

Instead of parentheses, periods are often used:

> We shall visit these cities in the following order: 1. New York, 2. Washington, 3. Chicago, 4. San Francisco.

Do not use parentheses to enclose words that are closely related to the preceding word.

> John Matthews (the clerk) gave him an application form. (Wrong)

John Matthews, the clerk, gave him an application form. (Right)

ELLIPSIS POINTS
(. . .) OR (* * *)

Three periods are used to indicate an ellipsis (the omission of a word or words) in a text. If the ellipsis is between two sentences, the period at the end of the first sentence is followed by the three points indicating the ellipsis, making four periods.

> The thunder was just beginning . . . there were dark clouds in the West. . . . We sat on the porch waiting for the rain to begin.

BRACKETS [ ]

Brackets are used:
To enclose explanatory material inserted in a quotation by some person other than the person quoted.

> In his last report, he explained to his advisor [Henry Drake] that the material needed extensive revision.

> Elaine said she would tell Charles [her brother] when she planned to arrive.

> The chairman [Mr. Walker] was late for the meeting.

> They never gave any indications [how Sam wished they had!] that they were dissatisfied.

HYPHEN (–)

When a word is divided at the end of a line, you must use a hyphen. Words of one syllable, such as

39

chair, clock, and friend, should never be divided. Do not divide a word with a silent *e*, such as *looked, toured, roamed.*

A word of two or more syllables may be divided at the end of a line according to either its derivation or its pronunciation. Division by pronunciation is more common. Because the rules regarding hyphenation vary so greatly, you should always consult a dictionary when in doubt.

There are some two-syllable words that should never be divided. These include words like *gentle, table, simple, flower, enough,* and *people.* In general, do not break any word of less than seven letters if you can possibly avoid it. Avoid breaking personal names, too.

Never divide a word so that only one letter is left on a line; as, *a-chieve, i-dentical, e-ventful, shadow-y.*

If possible, do not divide a word on two letters; as, *as-sure, re-fer, de-cide, loss-es, thick-en.*

When a word begins with a prefix, it should ordinarily be divided on the prefix.

<blockquote>
dis-like   mis-take   sub-marine
</blockquote>

When a word ends with a suffix, it may usually be divided on the suffix.

<blockquote>
repair-ing   condi-tion   south-ern
</blockquote>

With words ending in *-le,* the preceding consonant should be carried over to the next line.

<blockquote>
driz-zling   rum-bling   gar-gling
</blockquote>

Do not divide a word between two or more letters pronounced as one (a dipthong, *as, au, ou, ight, ow,* etc.): as, *la-udable, pla-intive, parti-al.* Divide as follows:

laugh-able   in-sight   re-nown

When vowels come together but are pronounced as separate syllables, the hyphens come between the vowels.

idi-osyncrasy   peri-odic   tri-umphant

Double consonants are commonly divided by a hyphen if a suffix has been added.

trim-ming   glad-den   put-ting

Verbs that end in a double consonant, however, should be divided between the complete root words and the suffix.

confess-ing   press-ure   stuff-ing

3 | Spelling and Capitalization

Every writer should give careful thought to spelling. Although an occasional misspelled word in a script would probably not of itself be a cause for the rejection of a manuscript, several misspelled words or errors in word usage would create a negative impression on editors.

Check in your dictionary any word about which you are in doubt. This will answer most spelling questions. Preferred spellings are listed first, and you should avoid alternate or British forms.

Some basic rules for spelling follow. If you pay careful attention to these, and use your dictionary whenever in doubt, there is no excuse for incorrect spelling.

Forming the plural

Most singular nouns form the plural by merely adding *s: book, books; table, tables.* Many others add *es,* particularly words ending in *s, ss, ch, sh,* and *z: bush, bushes; waltz, waltzes.*

Nouns ending in *y* preceded by a consonant form the plural by changing the *y* to *i* and adding *es: lady, ladies; country, countries.*

Nouns ending in *y* preceded by a vowel usually form the plural by adding *s: valley, valleys; journey, journeys; boy, boys.*

Nouns ending in *o* preceded by a vowel usually form the plural by adding *s; radio, radios; cameo, cameos.*

Nouns ending in *o* preceded by a consonant usually form the plural by adding *es: tomato, tomatoes; hero, heroes.* There are some exceptions to this rule; as, *piano, pianos; tango, tangos.*

The plural of compound words is usually formed by adding *s* to the most important part of the word only: as, *daughters-in-law, mothers-in-law.* If such words are not hyphenated, the *s* is usually added to the end of the word: *classrooms, crossroads.* Note, however, that in forming the possessive, the apostrophe (') always comes at the end of a compound word: *son-in-law's house; father-in-law's property.*

When spelling words with *ie* or *ei*, remember the old rule of *i* before *e* except after *c* or when sounded like *a* as in *neighbor* and *weigh.* Notable exceptions are *leisure, neither, foreign, weird,* and *height.*

Suffixes

Some of the basic rules for adding a suffix to a word follow, but as there are many exceptions and variations, it's always a good idea to consult a dictionary when you have any doubts about spelling.

1. Words ending in a double consonant, the last of which is not *c,* do not change before adding a suffix: *transact, transaction; wash, washable; wring, wringing.*

2. Words ending in a single consonant preceded by two or more accented vowels add a suffix without any change in the word: *wood, wooden; bargain, bargaining.*

3. Words ending in a single consonant preceded by a single vowel, accented on the last syllable, double the final consonant—*begin, beginning; occur, occurred; glad, gladden; fit, fitted*—unless the suffix begins with a consonant: *fit, fitness; glad, gladly.* Words ending in *x* are exceptions; they never double the consonant; *relax, relaxing.* The final consonant is not doubled if it is silent: *crochet, crocheting.*

4. Words ending in a single consonant, immediately preceded by one or more vowels, but *not* accented on the final syllable, remain unchanged before the suffix: *happen, happened; debit, debiting; differ, difference.* Exception: *transfer, transferred.*

5. There is a large group of words ending in *l* preceded by a single vowel that double the consonant in British spelling, but not in American spelling: *pencil, penciled* (American), *pencilled* (British); *travel, traveler* (American), *traveller* (British).

6. Words ending in silent *e* usually drop the *e* before adding a suffix beginning with a vowel; *fascinate, fascinating; continue, continuance; compose, composure; sale, salable.*

7. Words ending in silent *e* usually retain the *e* when adding a suffix beginning with a consonant: *encourage, encouragement; white, whiteness; wise, wisely.* (Exceptions: *judge, judgment; true, truly.*)

8. Words ending in *y* preceded by a consonant usually change the *y* to *i* before adding a suffix: *hurry, hurried; mercy, merciful; busy, busily.* Such words, how-

ever, do not make this change before the suffix *ing:* *hurry, hurrying; busy, busying; study, studying.* Exceptions: *pity, piteous; beauty, beauteous.*

9. Words ending in *y* preceded by a vowel usually keep the *y* before a suffix: *play, playing, playful; obey, obeying.*

10. Words ending in *c* add a *k* before a suffix that begins with *e, i,* or *y* if the *c* sound remains hard: *picnic, picnicking; panic, panicked; mimic, mimicking.* No *k* is added if the pronunciation of the *c* becomes soft; *critic, criticism; music, musician; physic, physician.*

To repeat again, never guess at the spelling of any word. Be especially careful of words that end in a suffix: *able* and *ible, ence* and *ance, ent* and *ant,* and *eed* and *ede* are often troublesome, unless you are an unusually good speller, or know the rules for adding these suffixes to various root words. But even then, the English language is full of exceptions! When in doubt, reach for your dictionary.

Hyphenated Words

A hyphen is used to join the parts of a compound word, though the trend today is moving away from the use of this mark. Many compound words, formerly hyphenated, are now written as one word. However, a hyphen should always be used when there is any chance of confusion resulting from its omission. Take, for example, the word *re-cover.* As written here, the word means *cover again.* Without the hyphen, the word would have an entirely different meaning *(to get back).*

In the use of hyphens, as in the use of other punctuation marks, be consistent throughout your manuscript. Some general guidelines for hyphens follow, but because these rules vary so much, it's best to consult your dictionary if you have any doubts about spelling.

Common Uses

1. To add a prefix to a word that begins with a capital letter:

> pro-British
> un-American
> Indo-European

2. To join compound numerals and compound words indicating fractional parts:

> thirty-five
> two-thirds
> three-fourths

3. To join words of a compound adjective:

> a well-to-do woman
> a healthy-looking baby
> a vice-presidential candidate

4. A hyphen is used to join certain combinations of words meant to be thought of as a single concept.

> father-in-law
> jack-in-the-pulpit
> jack-o'-lantern

5. To join a prefix to another word if the prefix ends in a vowel that is the same as the first letter in the base word.

> anti-intellectual (but *antisocial*)
> extra-alimentary (but *extrasensory*)

Exceptions: reexamine, reenter, reevaluate

6. To join certain prefixes such as *self* and *ex* to other words.

ex-governor
self-centered

Numbers

When do you spell out numbers, and when do you use figures? In most fiction or straight prose, where numbers are infrequent, they are usually spelled out. A good rule to follow is to write out round numbers (hundreds, thousands, and so on), and use figures for exact amounts of three or more digits. Here are some examples:

We have twenty-five dollars on hand.

The amount on hand is $25.26.

The company has three thousand employees.

The company employs 3822 workers.

In some writing, all numbers are spelled out; in others, figures are used for all numbers. Especially in newspapers, magazines, and technical publications, rules and styles vary: the important thing is to be consistent. If you spell out a number on one page, do not use a figure for that same number on the following page.

No matter what the number is, if it comes at the beginning of a sentence, spell it out. In the case of a long number, you may use the figure enclosed in parentheses following the written number. Sometimes you may want to reword a sentence so that the number will not appear at the beginning.

Abbreviations

Writers are often uncertain about the use of abbreviations or contractions.

In any literary writing, abbreviations should be used sparingly, if at all. Even such common abbreviations of *Co.* for *Company, Assn.* or *Assoc.* for *Association,* or *Dist.* for *District,* should not be used. Abbreviations should not ordinarily be used for honorary titles, or titles of royalty or academic or military rank; these should be written out, especially when the surname only is used; as, *Governor* Merrill, *Senator* Washburn, *Dean* Johnson. It is sometimes permissible to abbreviate a title when it precedes initials or a first name: *Capt.* John R. Jones, *Prof.* J. W. Clark. Abbreviated titles—*Mr., Mrs., Ms.,* and *Dr.*— are considered correct in practically all kinds of writing. It is also correct to use abbreviations of professional titles following a proper name: Nancy Hughes, *M.D.,* Walter Brown, *Ph.D.,* John T. Turner, *D.D.S.*

In general, do not abbreviate United States. In a footnote or a listing, it is usually acceptable to use the abbreviated form *U. S.;* as, *U. S.* Navy, *U. S.* Air Force. Names of states or territories should not be abbreviated.

Do not abbreviate the names of continents, countries, or particular locations; as, *So. Afr.* for *South Africa, N. Z.* for *New Zealand, West Ind.* for *West Indies, Gr. Plains* for *Great Plains,* and so on.

Do not abbreviate names (*Jas.* for *James, Chas.* for *Charles, Thos.* for *Thomas*). Write them in full.

Do not abbreviate the names of the days of the week, months of the year, or holidays.

In fact, in a literary work, abbreviations should not be used for proper names of any type.

In technical and scientific texts, manuals, and guidebooks, abbreviations are not only permissible but are often both logical and necessary. In other words, the type of writing under consideration really determines whether or not abbreviations are in good taste or of correct usage.

Though in some instances simplified spelling is used—*thru* for *through, catalog* for *catalogue*— these shortened forms have not yet come into general use, and most publishers and printers follow conventional usage.

Words Often Misspelled

abridgment
accede
accommodate
acknowledgment
acquiesce
adhere
adhesive
aggravate
alcohol
allege
apparent
argument
athlete
birthrate
bypass
calendar
cemetery
connoisseur
conscience

conscientious
conveyer (person)
conveyor (belt)
correspondence
counterfeit
definite
dependent
despair
deterrent
develop
diagramed
ecstasy
embarrass
endeavor
exceed
exercise
exhilarate
existence
exorbitant

fluorescent
foreword (preface)
gaiety
government
grateful
harass
heroes
hygiene
illegible
imaginary
impostor
independent
indict
indispensable
innocuous
inoculate
iridescent
irresistible
judgment
knowledgeable
liaison
license
lieutenant
liquefy
lose/loose
marshal
minuscule
misstate
naive
nickel
occurrence

omission
parallel
pastime
personal/personnel
phosphorous (adj.)
phosphorus (n.)
pique
plaque
pore/pour
privilege
prophecy (n.)
prophesy (v.)
questionnaire
rarefy
receipt
receive
recommend
reminiscence
repellent
restaurateur
resuscitate
rhyme
rhythm
salable
separate
stubbornness
supersede
surreptitious
surveillance
tranquillity
vaccinate

vacillate vicious
vacuum weird
vegetable yield
vengeance

Capitalization

Although there are some definite rules for capitalization, in actual practice the use of capitals varies considerably. Proper nouns—the names of persons and places—are *always* capitalized. Words that may be used as either common or proper nouns, or possibly adjectives, sometimes cause problems. The most important thing to keep in mind is to be consistent throughout any specific work. In general, the trend is moving toward using fewer capitals. Consult your dictionary when in doubt.

The following rules are in general use among editors, publishers, and printers.

Begin with a capital letter:
1. The first word of every complete sentence, as well as the first word of a phrase or clause that is an independent unit.

> Family problems weighed heavily on him.
>
> What a day! What a life! Why aren't you happy?

2. Countries, nationalities, states, cities, specific sections of the country, continents, rivers, etc.

> United States   Chinese
> Brazilian   Lake Erie
> Long Island Sound   New England

London	Toledo
The South	Africa
Atlantic Seaboard	Hudson Bay
Australia	Aleutian Islands
Pacific Ocean	Irish Sea
Missouri River	Rocky Mountains

State of Washington

3. Although the first word of each line of poetry in traditional forms is capitalized, modern poets (and many who were writing fifty years ago) create their own forms and conventions. Thus we have poets who use no capital letters (not only e. e. cummings) or, in other cases, follow no traditional pattern. Here is the most traditional form:

ART

In placid hours well-pleased we dream
Of many a brave unbodied scheme.
But form to lend, pulsed life create,
What unlike things must meet and mate:
A flame to melt—a wind to freeze;
Sad patience—joyous energies;
Humility—yet pride and scorn;
Instinct and study; love and hate;
Audacity—reverence. These must mate,
And fuse with Jacob's mystic heart,
To wrestle with the angel—Art.

—Herman Melville

4. The first word after a colon when it is the first word of a complete sentence.

He commanded her attention with his first words: "You may not leave this house."

A capital letter is not used when the text following a colon is a partial sentence or a series.

He wanted to tell his sister about the will: a document she was sure to protest.

5. The first word and all important words in the title of a book, poem, magazine, newspaper, play, song, opera, picture, statue, monument, etc.

A Chorus Line	*The Grapes of Wrath*
The Library of	Grant's Tomb
Congress	*Ode to a Grecian Urn*
The New Yorker	*The Washington Post*

6. *God* and all words used to indicate the Deity.

Almighty	Allah
Lord	Jehovah

7. Bible and Biblical terms and books or divisions of the Bible; also, the sacred writings of all religions.

Old Testament	the Koran
Leviticus	Lord's Prayer

But the word bible is not capitalized when it is used in the following manner:

The exercise manual was her bible.

Note also that certain pronouns referring to the Deity are capitalized; as His loving care, My Father, Thy mercy.

8. Names of planets, constellations, stars, and signs of the zodiac.

Venus	Aries
the North Star	Jupiter

9. The days of the week and months of the year.

Thursday   March

10. Holidays and special occasions.

Christmas   Fourth of July
Thanksgiving   Lincoln's Birthday

11. Trademark names.

Kleenex   Polaroid
Coca-Cola   Xerox

12. Political parties in noun or adjective forms.

Democrats   Democratic Party
Republicans   Socialists

13. Names of religious groups or denominations.

Christians   Catholics
Jews   Mormons
Methodists   Anglicans

14. Names of historical events, epochs, eras.

World War II   the Restoration
the Renaissance   the Middle Ages

15. Names of schools, societies, corporations, and other organizations.

Columbia University   Union Trust Com-
Knights of Columbus   pany

16. Titles of honor and respect.

President Clinton   Lady Astor
General Powell   Sir Anthony Hopkins

17. Abbreviations of titles following a proper name.

Nancy Hughes, M.D.   Alex Parker, Ph.D.
Ernest Stone, J.D.   Charles Hoyt, D.D.S.

18. The personal pronoun *I*.

19. Words referring to relatives (*Mother, Uncle,* etc.) when used in direct address.

Yes, *Father,* I shall be glad to go with you.
Aunt Linda, come to the phone, please.

But these words are not capitalized when used with a possessive pronoun or article.

David asked his mother for a ride to the beach.
My cousin from Kansas City is coming to visit.

20. *Army* and *navy* when referring to American or foreign military units.

the United States Army
the British Navy
the Air Force

21. The word *government* when referring to the United States Government or to a specific foreign government.

the Government of the United States
the Canadian Government

22. *Street, avenue, square, park, theater, building,* etc., only when referring by name to a specific place or building.

Fifth Avenue   Central Park
Harvard Square   Eiffel Tower

23. The article *the* when it is a definite part of a proper name or title:

The Honorable William Marshall
The Good Earth

24. Abbreviations such as *St.* for *Saint, Ste.* for *Sainte, Mt.* for *Mount,* etc.

St. Lawrence River
Sault Ste. Marie
Mt. Washington

Do not capitalize abbreviations of common nouns and minor parts of speech, except for special emphasis.

e.g.	i.e.
etc.	lb.
et al	cm.
cc.	kg.

4 Typing the Manuscript

A manuscript submitted for publication competes
with hundreds of others that cross editors'
desks, and it follows that the manuscript that is professional in appearance, easy to read, and free of
careless mistakes is likely to receive better attention
than those that do not meet these requirements. The
rules of manuscript preparation are simple, but they
should be followed carefully if you wish to have your
work•considered seriously by editors.

Tools and materials

The basic and most important rule of preparation
for any manuscript—from book-length works to fillers and sketches—is to type the manuscript double-
spaced, on standard 8½- × 11-inch white paper, on
one side of the page only. Handwritten manuscripts,
however legible, are not welcome; neither are manuscripts on colored paper or type in unusual type-
faces.

Whether you type your manuscript on a typewriter, word processor, or personal computer, you should be sure that the type is clear, clean, and legible. The ribbon or cartridge (black) should be in good condition, producing clear, legible type. Make sure your typewriter or printer remains in good working condition by having it cleaned and serviced regularly. If you are in the market for a new machine, consider such factors as work load and finances before choosing from the wide variety of equipment available: electric typewriters with self-correcting features; word processors; and personal computer systems. Once you decide how much you want to spend on new equipment, you should shop carefully, and, if possible, talk to other writers to see what sort of equipment they use and whether they're satisfied with it.

Word processors and computers that use word-processing software offer the most options for writers. Some writers, hesitant to use computers, use the word processor as a stepping stone between the typewriter and computer. Computers are capable of word processing, and can also accommodate bookkeeping and financing programs that may be of use to writers. Both word processors and computers are, of course, more expensive than typewriters, and you may decide that you don't need all the extra functions, or that your output and sales don't warrant making the investment. With a computer or word processor, you can insert or delete letters, spaces, or words, and move paragraphs, even entire pages, just by pressing a few keys, thereby eliminating the retyping, cutting, and pasting involved in revisions done on a conventional typewriter. If you decide that you want to change a character's name, you can instruct the computer to substitute the new name for the old one throughout the manuscript. You never have to worry about margins, because at the end of a line the machine moves, or "wraps," the word you are typing onto the next line. And you don't have to type the page number and title of your manuscript onto each sheet of paper; the word processor and computer do this automatically. Word processors and computers can take care of hyphenation, and "spell checker" and "grammar checker" options are also available. These functions are useful, though far from foolproof, and will not guarantee your manuscript is error-free. For instance, if you type a valid word—"he" instead of "the"—the spell checker won't notify you that it's not the word you want. Likewise, grammar checkers have limited capability. What this means is that you still have to proofread your manuscript carefully.

If you do decide to buy a personal-computer system, be sure your printer produces high-quality type. Another point to consider: If your printer uses tractor-fed paper (a continuous roll with perforations), always separate the sheets before submitting the work to an editor.

When you're satisfied that you have a machine that will produce clean copy, your next thought should be of paper—color, size, quality, and weight. An average grade, white bond paper with some rag content will generally prove satisfactory for the original copy (the one to be submitted for consideration). Weights of 14 lbs., 16 lbs., or even 20 lbs. for short manuscripts are acceptable. It's not necessary to buy expensive paper; there are many good mid-range brands available. While erasable paper has advantages for the typist, most publishers require that manuscripts be submitted on regular bond paper, since erasable paper smudges easily and can be difficult to read. Also avoid papers of extra heavy weight (such as parchment). If you submit photocopies, they should be clear and easy to read. And unless a specific request has been made to do so, you should **never** fax your manuscript to a publisher.

Other materials you'll need as you prepare your manuscript: pencils (including a colored pencil), pens, paper clips, eraser, correction fluid, scissors, tape, index cards, and scrap paper. When you're ready to send your manuscript to a publisher, you'll need other supplies, such as letter-size (#10) envelopes, large manila envelopes (9- x 12-inch), cardboard fillers, stamps, mailing labels, etc. If you're submitting a book-length manuscript, you'll need sturdy cardboard boxes (available from a stationer or photographic supply house).

Typing the Manuscript: General Rules

Whether you're typing a short story, book manuscript, play script, or poem, there are some basic rules that you must follow.

On the first page of your manuscript, type your name, address, and telephone number in the upper left- or right-hand corner. Some editors want your social security number listed under the phone number. About one-third down the page, type the title in capital letters, followed a line or two below by your name. Leave a three-line space and begin the text, indenting at least 5 spaces and preferably not more than 10 spaces from the left margin. Indent the first line of each paragraph the same number of spaces throughout the manuscript.

The following is an illustration of how the first page of the manuscript should be arranged:

John M. Smith   About 6,000 words
24 Lake St.   Copyright © 1994
Lexington, MA 02173
(617) 936-1234

A DAY IN THE COUNTRY

By John M. Smith

Although it is not essential, particularly for such material as short poems and fillers, you may type the *approximate* number of words in the manuscript in the upper right-hand corner of the first page opposite your name and address. To estimate the nearest round number of words, count the lines of a full typed manuscript page. Then, find the average number of words in a line. As words are of varying length, count the words in three or four full lines (including words such as *I, a, an, the,* etc.). Add these figures; then divide the total by the number of lines counted. This will give you the average number of words in a line. For instance, if three lines have 10, 8, and 12 words respectively, totaling 30 words, divide 30 by 3 (the number of lines counted), giving the answer 10, the average number of words in a line. Now multiply the number of lines on a full page by the average number of words in a full line and you will have the average number of words on a page. Multiplying this figure by the number of pages in the script will give you the approximate number of words in the whole manuscript. For example, if there are 25 lines on a full page and approximately 10 words in a full line, the average number of words on a page is 25 times 10, or 250 words. If there are 30 pages in the manuscript, the approximate number of words in the whole work is 250 times 30, or 7,500 words.

Beginning with the second page, number the pages consecutively in the upper right-hand corner. Type the author's surname or the title of the manuscript in full or abbreviated form after the page number. This helps identify a page that may become separated from the whole manuscript. (The first page does not need to be numbered.) Number the pages as you type them, in case the pages get out of order.

Margins on all manuscript pages should be uniform in width. Although there are no hard-and-fast rules concerning width, margins should be wide enough to give the page a neat, attractive appearance and to allow for an editor's instructions to the printer or proofreader's notations—generally, an inch to an inch–and–a–quarter for right- and left-hand margins. It's a good idea to allow a little more than an inch at the top and bottom of the sheet. Never start your typing at the very top of the page or run it clear to the bottom, and never run a line of type clear to the right-hand edge of the paper. Also, try to have about the same number of lines on each page, except, of course, first pages of chapters or those with special inserts. If you are working on a word processor, margins will be set, pages counted, and page numbers and headings typed automatically. (See sample page of story manuscript on page 75.)

Each paragraph should be set off by indenting the first line a certain number of spaces. Whether the paragraphs in a manuscript have one or a dozen sentences each, the identation should be the same throughout the work.

Any typed material that is to be printed in italics should be underlined. Titles of books, novels, collections of poetry, plays, magazines, newspapers, and motion pictures are customarily printed in italics. Titles of stories, articles, poems, and television and radio programs are usually enclosed in quotation marks.

Underline foreign words and phrases that are to be printed in italics. If the words are in common use and have become part of our language (such as liaison and rendezvous), there is no need to italicize them.

Italics are also used to emphasize a word or words in a text.

When including a short quotation in a manuscript, enclose it in quotation marks. If you are quoting more than one paragraph, put a quotation mark at the beginning of each paragraph and at the end of the last paragraph of the quoted section. (When the material appears in print, quotation marks are usually omitted, the quoted material indented and set in a smaller type than that used for the main body of the text.)

Permissions

Although quoting from published work in limited form (a paragraph or line or two) is generally considered "fair use" and does not require permission, there is no hard-and-fast rule as to just what constitutes fair use. There are, however, four factors to consider when trying to determine whether the use of certain material can be called "fair":

1. The purpose and character of the use: Is such use of a commercial nature or for nonprofit educational purposes?

2. The nature of the copyrighted work from which you wish to quote.

3. The proportion of the material to be quoted in relation to the length of the copyrighted work; for example, quoting even a few words or line from a poem may be considered an infringement of copyright, because such a quotation represents too large a percentage of the total work. This is particularly true of quoting song lyrics of *any* length, and permission of the copyright owner must *always* be requested (and often a fee paid).

4. The effect of the use on the potential market for or value to the copyrighted work. Brief quotations (usually up to 300 words) used in book reviews and in general criticisms of a work come under "fair use," for the most part.

Infringement of copyright is a serious matter, and if you are at all in doubt about whether a proposed quote from a copyrighted work meets fair-use guidelines, you should seek written permission from the copyright owner. When permission is necessary, it must be procured *in writing;* without such formal written permission, your use of the copyrighted material may be considered an infringement. In requesting permission, write to the original magazine or book publisher of the work you wish to quote, and be sure to enclose a self-addressed, stamped envelope. (Do not seek permission by telephone.) If the address of the publisher does not appear anywhere in the material, it may be found in *Literary Market Place,* available in most libraries. Be sure to state the exact extent of the material you wish to quote, and allow sufficient time for the publisher to check the status of the copyright, clear it with the author, etc. Granting of permission to duplicate copyrighted material is not a simple "yes" or "no" matter. If you wish to quote several sections of material from the same publisher for a specific project, you should submit a request for all of them at the same time. If the publisher of the copyrighted material requires a fee for its use, you will be responsible for it (unless, in the case of a book, your publisher has stipulated in the contract that he will assume a certain amount of permission fees).

Book Manuscripts

Follow the general rules for manuscript preparation, and also include a title page (not required for short manuscripts) on which the title is typed in capital letters about halfway down the page. On the line immediately below type the word "By" and your name. Only the title and author's name should appear on this page. The title page should not be counted as the first page of the manuscript.

The entire book manuscript should be numbered consecutively from the first page of text to the last— do not begin a new chapter with page one. Start each new chapter on a new page, typing the chapter number and chapter title (if any) about three inches from the top of the page. Leave two or three spaces and then proceed with the text.

Nonfiction books

A book-length manuscript will normally have a table of contents and often a preface, foreword, or introduction. Each of these preliminary parts (known as "front matter") should be on a separate sheet, with the proper heading typed in capital letters two or three spaces above the first line of the text. The typing on these pages, as on other pages of the manuscript, should be double-spaced and on one side only of the paper. The pages of each section should be numbered separately—for example, Preface 1, Preface 2, Preface 3, and so on. This form of page numbering will not, of course, appear in your published book; it is merely for the purpose of clarity during the process of publication. When published, small Roman numerals are usually used to indicate the page numbers of front and end matter.

Supplementary pages, or "end matter," such as an index or bibliography, should be treated in the same manner as front matter, with each section typed separately with its proper heading, and the pages of each section numbered separately. Here, as in other parts of the manuscript, the page number should be in the upper left- or right-hand corner of the page.

Fiction manuscripts

The basic rules for manuscript preparation also apply to short stories and novels. A novel should include a title page.

Dialogue should be typed in paragraph form, indented the same number of spaces as all other paragraphs.

> "Yes," he said, "we'll be there by eight o'clock."
> "Oh, Jerry," exclaimed Julie. "Can you come earlier and eat dinner with us?"

You may include a segment of dialogue within a paragraph or description or straight narrative. It is not customary to include the speeches of two different persons in the same paragraph.

After we had gone about thirty miles, Kate turned to me and said, "This doesn't look like the road to Bennington." We had just come within sight of a covered bridge at the foot of a hill.

"No, I don't remember any covered bridge," I answered. "Let's look at the map again." I pulled over to the side of the road and stopped the car.

"Now, that's strange." Kate was looking in the glove compartment where we always kept our maps. "It isn't here," she said.

Poetry

In typing poetry, center not only the title (with the author's name beneath) but the poem as a whole. This means, for one thing, that you should start the typing of a short poem fairly well down from the top of the page. If you are submitting more than one poem at a time, *type each one on a separate sheet no matter how short any one poem may be.* Always use a full-size sheet for each poem.

Center your poem according to its longest line; if any one line is so long that it throws the whole poem out of balance on the page, part of the line may be typed on the next line, indented four or five spaces. Type your poem single-space, double-spacing between stanzas. If your poem is short, you may type it double-space.

Quotations of two or more lines of poetry should be set off from the text. Center the quote on the page and set it line for line, always following the form used by the author:

> Keeping time, time, time,
> In sort of Runic rhyme,
> To the tintinnabulation that so musi-
> cally wells
> From the bells, bells, bells, bells,
> Bells, bells, bells.
> (Edgar Allan Poe, "The Bells")

If more than one line of a poem is run into the text, use a slash mark (/) to indicate line breaks:

> Mr. Jackson frequently repeated Tennyson's words, " 'Tis only noble to be good. / Kind hearts are more than coronets" ("Lady Clara Vere de Vere").

Greeting Card Verse

Greeting card companies often have their own specific requirements and guidelines for submitting ideas, finished verse, and artwork. The National Association of Greeting Card Publishers, however, gives the following general guidelines for submitting material: Each verse or message should be typed, double-spaced, on a 3″ × 5″ or 4″ × 6″ card. (If a verse is particularly long, it may be typed single-spaced; most greeting card companies prefer verses that are no longer than 8 lines.) Use only one side of the card, and be sure to put your name and address in the upper left-hand corner. Keep a copy of every verse or idea you send. (It's also advisable to keep a record of what you've submitted to each publisher.) Always enclose a stamped, self-addressed envelope, and do not send out more than ten verses or ideas in a group to any one publisher. Suggestions for illustrations and other notes may be typed at the bottom of the card containing the verse.

For other types of short material such as fillers, always use a full-size sheet for each item. Be sure also to have your name and address on each page when submitting two or more separate writings in one envelope.

Play Scripts

The format for typing scripts for the stage can vary—one theater or play publisher may have special requirements that playwrights submitting material are expected to follow. But there are two typing styles that are generally recognized as standard.

In the first style, character names, in capital letters, are centered on the page. The dialogue is typed double-spaced directly under the character name, with the first line indented about five spaces from the left-hand margin; second and subsequent lines are flush with the left-hand margin. Stage directions are typed single-spaced under the dialogue; they should be indented evenly about five spaces from the left-hand margin, and be underlined and enclosed in parentheses. If character names are used in stage directions, they should be in all capital letters, but not underlined. Brief stage directions may be inserted in the dialogue as needed, always enclosed in parentheses and underlined. (See sample on page 76.)

In the second style, character names are typed flush with the left-hand margin, followed by a colon, and then the dialogue. Subsequent lines of dialogue should be indented about five spaces from the left-hand margin. All dialogue is typed double-spaced. Long stage directions (single-spaced) should be indented about ten spaces from the left-hand margin, underlined, and enclosed in parentheses. Again, short stage directions may be inserted in dialogue as needed. (See page 77.)

The first pages of play scripts vary, depending on the length of the script and the complexity of settings, costumes, etc. For instance, the first page of a short script, such as a one-act play, will include title, name of author, list of characters, descriptions of scenes, notation of time and place, and so on, followed by the first part of the play itself. In a full-length play, on the other hand, it may take three or four pages for the list of characters, descriptions of acts and scenes, costumes, synopsis, and so on. See sample of the first page of a short script on page 78.

Television Scripts

Although the format for a television script may vary with the particular program involved, most television producers expect the pages of a script to be in two-column form, with one column—about half of the page—left blank. This blank space is for the use of the television director in making production notations of camera shots, lens sizes, camera position, and so forth. The blank column may be on either the right-hand or left-hand side of the page; a writer should check the producer's preference before submitting a script, when he writes for a release form. In almost every case, television producers require writers to attach signed release forms to their scripts. The release form is a waiver that frees the producer from any liability for your manuscript. You can obtain the release form by sending a self-addressed, stamped envelope to the producer to whom you will be submitting material.

In a television script, the names of characters are capitalized and centered above the dialogue. Stage directions, which may also be in capital letters, are typed flush with the left-hand margin. All dialogue should be indented about five spaces from the left-hand margin. (See sample on page 79.) At the beginning of your script, include a list of the names of characters and a brief description of each one, as well as an indication of the number of sets in the script and a short description of each.

Checking and correcting your manuscript

Before typing the final copy of your manuscript, read over the entire script and correct errors in grammar, spelling, capitalization, or punctuation; verify statements of facts, statistics, quotations, names of real persons, dates; and check the work as a whole for inconsistencies. Sloppy presentation and inadequate copyediting on your part are the marks of an amateur, and will jeopardize your chances of having your manuscript accepted by a publisher.

When you mention the title of a book, story, article, or poem, always give the source of the reference. Who wrote the book you refer to? Who was the publisher, and when was it published? In what publication did you see that article—and in what issue? In what work was the character mentioned—who were the author and publisher? These are the sorts of questions your publisher will expect you to answer.

If there are a few minor corrections to make in

your manuscript—for instance, you may want to add or transpose a word or phrase, correct a typographical error, or italicize a word—you may simply write them in, using the standard proofreader's marks (see pages 80 and 81). A page with several changes and additions should be retyped. The clearer the copy, the more professional it will appear to the editor.

Proofreading

After your manuscript has been accepted and set into type, it must be proofread before it is published. In most cases, you won't see the proof of a short manuscript that has been accepted for publication by a magazine, but you'll usually be asked to read and correct a book manuscript, first in galley proof (the first set of proofs, set in long strips), and sometimes, but not generally, in page proof (a proof that is shown page-by-page in the form it will be in the published book).

The proof that the publisher sends you will have the proofreader's corrections marked on it. The original manuscript will usually be returned with the proof, so that you can check the proof against the copy. Proofread carefully for technical errors in grammar, spelling, sentence structure, word usage, and punctuation, referring to specific sections of this book when necessary. Check and verify all names of persons or places, dates, quotations, or references of any kind, and don't rely on your memory for accuracy. *This is essential,* even though the material will be carefully proofread by your publisher's staff. It is very easy to overlook a point here and there as the material goes through the various stages from typed manuscript to final publication.

Most publishers use a particular dictionary for spelling and reference and may change your spelling unless you clearly indicate a preference for a specific authority. If you do have a preference, inform the publisher of this fact before, not after, the manuscript has been put in type. Changes in text after it is in type are very costly.

Make your corrections (termed "author's alterations") on the proof in colored pen or pencil, to distinguish them from the corrections of the publisher's proofreader. Use standard proofreader's marks and be sure to print clearly, so the printer won't have to waste time trying to decipher your marks. Under no circumstances should you erase any proofreader's marks or write corrections over any passage in the proof. Make all corrections in the margins of the proof. If you want to make more than one correction per line, mark them in the margin in the order that they are to be made in the line, reading left to right, and separating them with a vertical line or slash.

Sometimes what may appear to be a very simple correction may require the resetting of a whole paragraph or page. Insertion or deletion of a short passage or even a few words may necessitate extensive (and expensive) resetting. If you are adding a few words to a line, try to make a deletion of the same number of words in the same line or the next one or two, so that the least possible number of lines will have to be reset. If you can make your additions or deletions at the end of a paragraph, so much the better. To estimate the length of additional new text, count *all* letters and spaces carefully.

Keep in mind that corrections are expensive, and if possible, all necessary changes should be made in galley proof. It is a much simpler—and considerably less expensive—matter to have corrections made while material is in this form than after it is made up into pages.

Return the corrected set of proofs and the original manuscript to the publisher promptly. If you have any questions about corrections, take them up with the publisher at once, so that further corrections may be avoided.

Sample page of a story manuscript:

Charles Dickens   -3-   A Christmas Carol

"A merry Christmas, uncle! God save you!" cried a cheerful voice. It
was the voice of Scrooge's nephew, who came upon him so quickly that this
was the first intimation he had of his approach.

"Bah!" said Scrooge, "Humbug!"

He had so heated himself with rapid walking in the fog and frost, this
nephew of Scrooge's, that he was all in a glow; his face was ruddy and
handsome; his eyes sparkled, and his breath smoked again.

"Christmas a humbug, uncle!" said Scrooge's nephew. You don't mean
that, I am sure!"

"I do," said Scrooge. "Merry Christmas!   What right have you to be merry?
You're poor enough."

"Come, then, returned the nephew gaily. "What right have you to be so
dismal? What reason have you to be morose? You're rich enough."

Scrooge, having no better answer ready on the spur of the moment said,
"Bah!" again; and followed it up with "Humbug."

"Don't be cross, uncle!" said the nephew.

"What else can I be," returned the uncle, "when I live in such a world of
fools as this? Merry Christmas! Out upon merry Christmas! What's Christmas
time to you but a time for paying bills without money; a time for finding
yourself a year older, but not an hour richer; a time for balancing your books
and having every item in 'em through a round dozen of months presented dead
against you? If I could work my will," said Scrooge indignantly, "every idiot
who goes about with 'Merry Christmas' on his lips should be boiled with his own

Samples of two different styles of play scripts:
(Style 1)

> RONNIE
>
> Say, Julie (<u>Pointing</u>), do you notice how these clothes
> are moving on the line?
>
> JULIE
>
> It's the wind.
>
> RONNIE
>
> What wind? There isn't a breath of air stirring.
>
> JULIE
>
> That's strange. (<u>Suddenly</u>) Ronnie! Look!
>
> RONNIE
>
> What's the matter?
>
> JULIE
>
> My blouse and skirt are gone!
>
> RONNIE
>
> Oh, Julie, for heaven's sake. I thought it was something
> serious.
>
> JULIE
>
> It <u>is</u> serious. That was my good blouse, and my best skirt.
> I'm telling you, there's something really weird about all this.
> I'm half scared.
>
> RONNIE
>
> Now, there you've said a mouthful! Scared is right. You're
> scared of everything. You're scared of your mother, you're scared of
> your dad, you're scared of my whole family, and now you're scared of
> this clothesline! Come on, let's get these clothes down so you can
> run in the house and hide.
>
> > (<u>On this speech, RONNIE takes down the center sheet,
> > revealing the figure of a GHOST behind it</u>. GHOST
> > is wearing a Shakespearean costume, but is in the
> > <u>act of putting on a man's shirt</u>. <u>The shirt is un-
> > buttoned</u>. Over his arm, the GHOST <u>carries JULIE's
> > missing blouse and skirt</u>. At the sight of him,
> > JULIE <u>screams and runs to RONNIE for protection</u>.)

(Style 2)

RONNIE (Pointing): Say, Julie, do you notice how these clothes are moving on the line?

JULIE: It's the wind.

RONNIE: What wind? There isn't a breath of air stirring.

JULIE: That's strange. (Suddenly) Ronnie! Look!

RONNIE: What's the matter?

JULIE: My blouse and skirt are gone!

RONNIE: Oh, Julie, for heaven's sake. I thought it was something serious.

JULIE: It is serious. That was my good blouse, and my best skirt. I'm telling you, there's something really weird about all this. I'm half scared.

RONNIE: Now, there you've said a mouthful! Scared is right. You're scared of everything. You're scared of your mother, you're scared of your dad, you're scared of my whole family, and now you're scared of this clothesline! Come on, let's get these clothes down so you can run in the house and hide.

> (On this speech, RONNIE takes down the center sheet, revealing the figure of a GHOST behind it. GHOST is wearing a Shakespearean costume, but is in the act of putting on a man's shirt. The shirt is unbuttoned. Over his arm, the GHOST carries JULIE's missing blouse and skirt. At the sight of him, JULIE screams and runs to RONNIE for protection.)

JULIE: Ronnie! Ronnie! It's a ghost! Save me! Save me!

Sample first page of a short play script:

```
                    CLOTHES ENCOUNTERS

                       by L. Press


        Characters

   RONNIE, 28, self-confident and well-dressed

   JULIE, 25, Ronnie's girlfriend.  Immature and vain


   TIME:  Late afternoon, the present.

   SETTING:  Julie's backyard in Hoboken.

   AT RISE:  RONNIE and JULIE are standing by the clothesline.

   JULIE:  It's a beautiful day for drying clothes, isn't it, Ronnie?
```

Sample page of a television script:

FADE IN:

INT: COACH'S KITCHEN--NIGHT

It's a modern garden-apartment kitchen
in total disorder. It's littered with toys,
crayons, books, dirty dishes, etc.

Kenny, a seven-year-old, in the middle of
this mess, is having a tantrum. Jamie tries
to cope with him.

                KENNY

      I don't want to stay with you! I want
      my Daddy!

                JAMIE
      I told you, he'll be back in a couple
      of hours. . .Now, why don't you finish
      your supper?

                KENNY
      I want to eat <u>out</u> for my birthday.
      He promised.

                JAMIE
      Kenny, you'll celebrate with him
      tomorrow. Come on now, finish your
      sandwich.

Kenny pushes the plate away and it falls to
the floor.

                KENNY
      I want my Daddy! I don't want to stay
      with you!

He kicks his way to a corner and turns his
back on Jamie. Jamie looks at him, then
takes a deep breath.

                JAMIE
      Tough!

Jamie ignores him. He finds a carton and
begins a clean-up job, throwing the toys and
books into the carton. Gradually Kenny turns
around and, in spite of himself, is fascinated
by Jamie's perfect aim as he pitches objects
into the proper receptacles.

                    DISSOLVE TO:

INT: KITCHEN-NIGHT.

Standard proofreader's marks:

MARK	EXPLANATION	EXAMPLE
℮	Take out character indicated.	℮ The proof.
∧	Left out, insert.	h The proof.
#	Insert space.	# Theproof.
X	Broken letter.	X The proof.
eq#	Even space.	eq# A good proof.
‿	Less space.	‿ The proof.
⁔	Close up; no space.	⁔ The proof.
tr	Transpose.	tr A proof good.
wf	Wrong face.	wf The proof.
lc.	Lower case.	lc. The Proof.
ꞌꞌ	Broken scoring.	ꞌꞌ The proof.
SC	Solid scoring.	SC The proof.
≡ & ═	Capitals and small caps.	The proof.
caps. ≡	Capitals.	caps The proof.
italcaps ≡	Italic caps.	italcaps The proof.
ital. —	Italic.	ital. The proof.
rom.	Roman.	rom. The proof.
bf. ⌇⌇⌇	Bold face.	bf The proof.
stet.	Let it stand.	stet The proof.
cc	See copy.	cc He proof.
SP	Spell out.	SP King Geo
¶	Start paragraph.	¶ read. The
No ¶	No paragraph; run in.	No ¶ marked. The proof.
⌐⌐	Raise.	The proof.
⌐⌐	Lower.	The Proof.
[	Move left.	[The proof.

80

MARK	EXPLANATION	EXAMPLE
⟧	Move right.	The proof. ⟧
‖	Align type.	‖ Three men. ‖ Two women.
∧ ⊙	Insert period.	⊙/The proof∧
⟨∧⟩	Insert comma.	⟩/The proof∧
⟨∴⟩	Insert colon.	:/The proof∧
⟨⟩	Insert semicolon.	⟩/ The proof∧
ⱽ	Insert apostrophe.	ⱽ The boy˅s arm
ⱽ ⱽ	Insert quotation marks.	⟨⟨ ⟩⟩ The ˅proof˅ of
=/	Insert hyphen.	=/ A well known∧
⟨9⟩	Insert inferior character.	∧ $A_9 + B_9 = C$∧
ⱽ⁹/	Insert superior character.	ⱽ $A^9 + B^9 = C$˅
!/	Insert exclamation mark.	!/Prove it∧
?/	Insert question mark.	?/Is it good∧
Au: ⓠ	Query for author.	ⓠ proof˜was read by∧
[/]	Insert brackets.	[/] ∧See Eq. 3(a)∧
(/)	Insert parentheses.	(/) The proof∧ 1∧
⊢⊣N	Insert 1-en dash.	⊢⊣N 1922⊣1958∧
⊢⊣M or ⊢⊣	Insert 1-em dash.	⊢⊣M A proof∧First
⊢2⊣M	Insert 2-em dash.	⊢2⊣M Taylor∧
▢	Indent 1 em.	▢ The proof.
⊞	Indent 2 ems.	⊞ The proof.
▧	Indent 1 en (1/2 em).	▧ The proof.
⟧ ⊏	Center copy	⟧ The ⊏ ⟧ proof ⊏

81

5 || Supplementary Material: Footnotes, Bibliographies, and Indexes

There are several aspects of preparing a manuscript that apply only to nonfiction books of an academic, technical, or instructional nature, primarily *footnotes, bibliographies,* and *indexes.* Many publishers of this type of book have their own special forms and guidelines for the preparation of footnotes and bibliographies, and very often indexes are prepared by professional indexers usually selected by the publisher. For simpler books of a nontechnical nature, however, you may prefer to do the index (following the generally accepted form).

Footnotes

A footnote — explanatory material that gives the source of a fact, quote, or other reference — is placed at the foot of the page on which it appears. (Although traditionalists prefer footnotes, "endnotes," which are like footnotes but are placed all together at the end of the book or article, are also widely used.)

Word-processing software makes it easy to add footnotes to your manuscript; the software automatically reserves space at the bottom of each page for footnote text, and renumbers footnotes and reference marks whenever you add, delete, or move them around.

When you prepare your manuscript on a typewriter, insert the footnote immediately following the part of the text to which the note refers. In this way, you won't have to worry about leaving the correct amount of space at the bottom of that page. The footnote should be set off from the rest of the material by a line above and below it. About one space under the last sentence of the material to be footnoted, type a straight line across the page. Leave a space, then type the footnote. Type another line beneath the note, then double-space and continue with the text.*

---

*Here is an illustration of how a footnote should appear in a *typewritten* manuscript.

Reference to a footnote should be indicated by a superior figure, [1] which is a number raised just above a printed line, or by an asterisk (*) following the last word to which the note refers. Footnote numbers in the text follow any punctuation marks (except a dash) and are placed outside a closing parenthesis. In typing the footnote, the superior figure or asterisk should precede the note.

In a book manuscript, number the notes 1, 2, 3, 4, and so forth, right through a chapter; then start with the figure 1 again for the next chapter. In a short manuscript, it is all right to number the footnotes 1, 2, 3, 4, and so on, straight through the manuscript.

There are various kinds of footnotes. One type of note may be in the form of a simple statement or explanation, or even a single word. Another may give the name of an author or a publisher, or the title of a work, with a page number. Still another may give the name of an author, title of a work, publisher, date of publication, and so on. Here are a few illustrations:

1. David Kirby, *Writing Poetry: Where Poems Come From and How to Write Them.* The Writer, Inc., pp. 25-27.
2. Elizabeth George, "A Novel By Any Other Name," *The Writer,* January, 1994, p. 11.
3. See *The Mother Earth News,* April 1993, p. 42.

It is essential to keep an accurate record of all footnotes on a separate set of index cards.

Bibliography

A bibliography, which appears in the section of the book preceding the index, is a list of citations and references that the author has made in the text of a nonfiction work. The form may vary according to the complexity of the book or the publisher's preference, but generally, each entry includes the last name of the author or editor, followed by his or her first name or initials. The title of the referenced work comes next (if a book, it should be underlined when typed, as it will appear in italics in the printed version; or if typed on a computer, simply formatted into italic type). If the reference is an article, part of a long work, a short story, poem, or essay, it should be enclosed in double quotation marks. Also included, following the author's name and the title of the work cited, are the name of the publisher, place and date of publication, edition, if specified, volume number, and other identifying information.

The listings should be arranged alphabetically by the last name of author or editor. If more than one work by the same author or editor is included in your bibliography, a three-em dash may be used to represent the author or editor's name after the first entry. If the same *work* is cited, there is no need to repeat the title and publishing information after the first time; ibid. can be used instead.

Here is a sample of some typical bibliographical references:

Doerr, Harriet. *Consider This, Señora.* New York: Harcourt Brace & Company, 1993.

Kenison, Katrina, Ed. *The Best American Short Stories 1993.* Boston: Houghton Mifflin, 1993.

"Methodism," *The Columbia Encyclopedia, Fifth Edition,* p. 1759. New York: Columbia University Press, 1993.

Morrison, Toni. *Song of Solomon.* New York: Signet, 1978.

———. *Tar Baby.* New York: NAL, 1982.

Olds, Sharon. "The Language of the Brag," *The Pittsburgh Book of Contemporary American Poetry,* p. 199. Pittsburgh: University of Pittsburgh Press, 1993.

Ostriker, Alicia Suskin. "A Meditation in Seven Days," ibid., p. 208.

Plimpton, George, Ed. *Writers at Work: The Paris Review Interviews. Ninth Series.* New York: Penguin, 1992.

Stumbo, Bella. "Sex, Lies, & Stereotypes," *Lear's,* November, 1993.

The Index

You have written a nontechnical book for which you want to prepare a simple index, including the main topics discussed, names and authors of books or articles mentioned in your text, and terms that are important and have been defined.

First, working from page proofs (because it is only at this stage that you have the page numbers), underline in colored pen or pencil or highlighter pen each item you wish to include in your index. When you have gone through the text completely in this way, put each underlined entry on a separate 3″ × 5″ index card, with its page number. In the case of a book or article title, be sure to have a separate entry for the title (by the first main word, not articles like *an* or *the*) and another for the author.

Be sure to check back on each entry for accuracy in spelling and page number. Within each entry mark the *key* word (usually a noun in any item that is not a proper name or book title).

Your next step is to arrange the cards in alphabetical order by key word for topics, titles and authors.

Use a minimum of cross references for main categories. For example, you might have a main entry for *word processing* under *w*. Other related entries, like *IBM, software, disks,* etc., you may wish to include under *word processing* and possibly *computers*. But for your simple index, don't break the categories down too fine.

In the course of alphabetizing the cards, be consistent. For instance, there are variations in the way names beginning with *Mc* or *Mac* are alphabetized.

One form is to treat *Mc* and *Mac* as if they were both *Mac.* The proper order for the following names would in that case be *McAdams, MacCormack, Macdonald, McManus, MacNiff.* If you use another model in which the names are arranged in a strictly alphabetical order *(MacCormack, Macdonald, MacNiff, McAdams, McManus),* be sure to do so consistently throughout to avoid confusion.

Similarly, when *d', de, de la, du, la, van, von, van der* (either in lower case or in capital letters) precede the surname but *are part of it,* alphabetize by the name that the people are known by. Thus:

de Gaulle, Charles Andres
De Koven, Reginald
De la Mare, Walter John
de la Roche, Mazo
de l'Orme, Philibert
de Mille, Agnes
De Quincey, Thomas
d'Erlanger, Baron Frederic A.
Du Barry, Comtesse
Du Gard, Martin
La Farge, John
Lafayette, de, Marquis
La Guardia, Fiorello
Van Buren, Martin
Van de Graaf, Robert Jemison
van Dyke, Henry
Van Rensselaer, Martha

If you have an entry that properly would by its spelling be interfiled with such a list, it should be put in its alphabetical place, as in:

> Van Doren, Carl
> *Vanity Fair*
> Van Loon, Hendrik Willem

All titles of books, motion pictures, and plays in the index should be italicized, and would therefore be underlined in your typed copy. Names of articles, stories, and television shows should be enclosed in double quotation marks.

When there are two or more entries that are the same but on different pages, include all page numbers under the key word entry. For example: *Plot, 16, 32, 87.*

When there are two or more entries with the same surname but different first names, arrange them alphabetically by first name:

> Evans, Henry J.
> Evans, Walter P.

If the publisher does not have an index guideline, follow a published model that you like—but to repeat, be consistent.

When all of your cards are alphabetically arranged, checked, and page numbers combined for the same *key word* entry, type the index in list form, in a single column. Double space between entries, triple space between each section beginning a new letter (i.e., A, B, C, etc.).

Here are a few sample indexes:

6 | Submission and Marketing

You have finished your manuscript—story, article, or book—and are ready to submit it for publication. It is in content, form, and style, the best you can make it: You have checked it for grammar, punctuation, wording, sentence structure. It is typed (whether on a typewriter or a word processor) according to accepted and required format—double-spaced, clean copy, with your name, page number and identifying partial or full title in the corner. Now what?

If you have not written your manuscript with a particular market in mind, you must select an appropriate market. Though it is obvious that there is no point in sending a short story to a magazine that never publishes fiction, an article on cross-country skiing to a confession magazine, or a book of poetry to a publisher that brings out only novels and how-to books, there are more subtle differences in a magazine or book publisher's editorial focus and tone that you should be aware of.

Before submitting material to magazines, read the market lists in *The Writer* and *The Writer's Handbook*. Study back issues of a publication to learn its editorial scope and range, length and type of material used, and the audience it wishes to satisfy. Read the articles, stories, even advertisements. If you can't find sample copies of the magazine at the library or on the newsstands, write to the editor, asking the price of a sample copy. Many publications also have printed sheets of editorial guidelines describing the types of manuscripts they publish, and their required submission procedure; send a note asking for a copy and enclose a stamped, self-addressed envelope. In the case of book publishers, again, study the market lists carefully—they give the names and addresses of companies, descriptions of types of books in which they're interested, length requirements, submission requirements, and names of the editors to whom material should be sent. In the course of trying to find a market for your book, you should keep up with trends in book publishing by reading such trade magazines as *Publishers Weekly*, available in your library, as well as the book pages of magazines and newspapers. Also, study the competition—what books have you read lately that you like, and who published them? Your aim is to find a publisher who brings out the kind of novel you've written, or is interested in the subject of your nonfiction book. You should also check in *Subject Guide to Books in Print* (also in the library) to see if there are other books on the same subject as yours. If there are, how is yours different from them? It's to your advantage to find the right publisher for your book, and the extra effort that you put into research *before* you send out your manuscript should pay off.

Of course, even if you are thoroughly familiar with the publisher to which you are submitting your material, there is always a chance that your work will be rejected for reasons out of your control: the magazine or book publisher may be overstocked, or it may be that the publisher has recently bought or published a manuscript on the same subject as yours. If this happens, send your manuscript out again immediately to another likely market. Publishing history is full of stories of manuscripts that have been rejected several times before achieving publication—some going on to become best sellers. As your manuscript makes the rounds of publishers, some of the pages may get crumpled or torn. Always retype damaged pages.

Do you need an agent?

Many writers feel that they cannot market their work on their own, that they must have an agent submit their manuscripts for them. Agents do provide worthwhile and vital services for authors, but most agents will not take on the work of beginners. Because reputable agents work entirely on a commission basis (generally earning 15 percent of the amount received for the sales of an author's work), they most often work with experienced writers who sell regularly. But if a writer has had some success marketing short items (stories, articles, etc.) on his own, an agent may be willing to risk representing a relatively new but talented author.

It is a realistic fact of life today that novels and book-length nonfiction can often be more successfully marketed by an established literary agent who keeps up with changing market needs, specific requirements and demands of particular editors and publishers, and who can, therefore, successfully negotiate contracts on behalf of a writer. It is also interesting to note, however, that not all successful authors have agents, preferring to handle all sales and negotiations themselves.

If you do decide to seek the services of a literary agent, select one with care, and beware of agents who charge fees to read and edit your manuscripts. Consult the list of reputable agents available for a $5 check and a self-addressed envelope with two first-class stamps from the Association of Authors' Representatives (10 Astor Pl., 3rd Fl., New York, NY 10003). Send an agent a query describing your work, your publishing credits, and any special qualifications you have for writing on a particular subject. In many instances an agent will approach you after seeing your work in print.

If you are a free-lance writer working without a literary agent, you must be familiar with the submission procedures required by various publications or book publishers *before* you send your manuscript out.

Queries

Many magazines and some book publishers are willing to read complete, unsolicited manuscripts, and in these cases, you may simply enclose a covering letter with the manuscript (see sample on page 97). More often that not, however, you'll find that publishers prefer—or even require—that writers query them first, especially for nonfiction, and increasingly even for novels. Of course, submission guidelines vary, depending on the type of material you've written and the publisher to whom you're sending it, and you should be sure to follow specified guidelines closely.

In the case of articles, your query letter should briefly describe the main points you intend to discuss in the course of your article, the proposed length, and any special qualifications you may have for dealing with the subject of the proposed piece. For a book-length nonfiction manuscript, your proposal may include an outline and sample chapter(s), but of course, this depends on what the publisher you've selected wants to see initially. As for novels, publishers now most often require a synopsis briefly describing the plot, characters, and setting of your book, as well as sample chapters. If the editor is interested in your proposal as described in your query, he will invite you to submit more material—a detailed outline, summary, or the complete manuscript.

You usually do not need to query magazine editors before submitting short stories, poetry, fillers, or other short material. Some publishers of poetry specify in editorial guidelines that you may submit poems in batches (up to 10 at a time, for example)—follow their instructions exactly. Play submission procedures vary widely, with some theaters willing to consider completed scripts, others requesting a package that includes a cast list, set description, synopsis, resumé, and so forth. As with all other submissions, check with the publisher or theater director before putting anything into the mail. Failure to follow preferred submission procedures may hurt your chances of acceptance. And remember: **Always enclose stamped, self-addressed envelopes with all queries, proposals, and manuscripts submitted.**

Writers understandably want to get a response

from publishers or editors as soon as possible. But there are certain acceptable—and unacceptable—procedures that free-lance writers should be aware of. Multiple queries (sending a *query* to more than one publisher simultaneously) are becoming increasingly accepted, and most editors will consider such submissions. But sending complete copies of the same manuscript to more than one publisher at the same time—called multiple or simultaneous submissions—is not a generally accepted practice. Most editors aren't willing to invest the time it takes to read an entire manuscript unless they know they are getting the exclusive chance to consider it for publication.

Mailing requirements

Manuscripts may be sent by first-class mail, or—less expensively— by *Special Fourth Class Rate—Manuscript*. In general, the postal regulations for this rate are as follows:

1. Manuscripts for books and periodicals may be mailed at the *Special Fourth-Class Rate*. This is a fixed rate per pound or fraction of a pound, without regard to zone.

2. For current postage rates for *Special Fourth-Class Rate—Manuscript,* consult your post office.

3. Envelopes and packages must be marked on the outside, *Special Fourth-Class Rate—Manuscript.*

4. Manuscripts marked *Special Fourth-Class Rate—Manuscript* may be insured, with a return receipt requested at the post office when mailed.

5. Letters may not be enclosed with manuscripts at the above manuscript postage rates. If you include a letter, state on the outside of the package that first-

class material is enclosed, and place additional first-class postage for it on the envelope.

It is not necessary to use any special delivery service to mail your manuscript. An unsolicited manuscript sent in this manner does not receive special attention.

You may send the manuscript pages loose, or enclose them in a lightweight paper folder, with the pages held together by paper clips; don't use clamps or staple the pages together. Mail the manuscript in a large, sturdy manila envelope; you may also protect your material with a thin piece of cardboard, if you wish. (A manuscript under ten pages may be folded once or twice, depending on the type of envelope used.) Be sure to enclose a stamped, self-addressed envelope for the return of your manuscript in case it is not accepted. (If you do not wish to have the manuscript returned, you may simply enclose an SASE or self-addressed, stamped postcard for the editor's response.) Postage for the return of a work submitted to a foreign market may be in stamps of the country to which the material is being sent (if available) or in International Reply Coupons, which may be purchased from your local post office.

Book-length manuscripts should be mailed flat and loose in a cardboard box (a typing paper box is a good choice), or in a sturdy mailing bag. If you wish to have your book manuscript returned, be sure that the self-addressed mailer you enclose is large enough, and has sufficient postage attached. Do not place stamps in a separate envelope or staple them to the front of the manuscript. If the postage should somehow become detached from the manuscript, your material might not be returned to you.

You may include a brief cover letter with your manuscript, telling the editor about your publication credits, and any relevant qualifications you have for writing on a particular subject. Here is a sample:

Mr. Edward Allen, Articles Editor
XYZ Magazine
100 Park Avenue
New York, NY 10017

Dear Mr. Allen:

I am enclosing for your consideration an article entitled "Make the Most of Your Talent."

A teacher of sociology at Westwood College for the past two years, I have written a regular column on personal success for *The Westwood Weekly Chronicle*.

If you do not find this article suitable for publication, please return it in the enclosed self-addressed, stamped envelope.

Sincerely,

Once your package is complete, clearly print or type the name and address of the publisher to which the material is being sent, and be sure to put your name and address in the upper left-hand corner. Attach sufficient postage, as described on page 95.

Always keep a copy of your manuscript. If you are submitting artwork, photos, or slides (and you should do so only after such material has been specifically requested by an editor), be sure the package is properly insured. **Never** mail irreplaceable slides or photos.

Records

Keep a record of your submissions: title of manuscript, market to which submitted, date mailed, date accepted or returned, date published, etc. Notations of this kind may be made on a sheet attached to the copy of your manuscript you keep, or on the copy itself, or a card file may be kept, with a separate card for each of your manuscripts in circulation, with essential information, and filed by title.

Reporting time

No definite statement may be made concerning the length of time that may elapse between the date of submission and the date a report is made or a manuscript returned. Even for a short story or article, major magazines may take two to three months to respond. For a book-length manuscript (currently, as noted earlier, submitted only if the publisher asks to see the complete work in response to your query), a three months' minimum is not unusual.

Always allow an editor plenty of time to read your material. Don't telephone a publishing office for a report. Bear in mind that editors have many manuscripts besides yours to read and consider. If you do not receive a report or the return of a manuscript within what seems to you a reasonable length of time, write a courteous note inquiring about the status of your manuscript.

If you are submitting material of a timely nature, submit it well in advance of the date when it should appropriately be published. Holiday-related material, for example, should be submitted at least six months early, as magazines need several months' "lead time."

7 | Rights and Copyrights

What types of writing may be copyrighted? How do you apply for copyright? How long is your work protected? In whose name should a copyright be issued?

These are questions which you as a writer will legitimately ask when you offer a piece of your writing for publication. Here, in brief form, are some of the basic answers that you should know, whether you write full time or part time. For more complicated copyright questions, you should write directly to the Copyright Office (Register of Copyrights, Library of Congress, Washington, DC 20559), consult a copyright lawyer, or your agent, if you have one.

What is Copyright?

Copyright laws of the United States protect "original works of authorship" including literary, dramatic, musical, artistic, and certain other "intellectual" works. The protection is available for both published and unpublished works. Under the law, copyright is secured *automatically* when the work is set down for the first time in written or recorded form. What this means to you as a writer or "creator" of a work is that you own and control its publication and use.

Several categories of material are generally not protected by copyright, including speeches or performances that have not been written or recorded; titles, names, and slogans; ideas, concepts, principles or devices, as distinguished from descriptions, explanations, or illustrations; and works consisting *entirely* of information that is common property and containing no original authorship, such as standard calendars, material from public documents or other common sources, etc. (A note about titles: Although they cannot be copyrighted, if a work by a specific title becomes a best seller or is in some other way commercially successful, it would be unwise to use the same title for any related work with which it might be confused.)

Copyright Notice

Should a copyright notice be put on unpublished works, particularly on those that are to be submitted to publishers? Although technically such a notice is not required on unpublished works, it's a good idea to write or type a copyright notice on your manuscripts before you submit them for publication. The copyright notice should include the following three elements:

- The symbol © (letter C in a circle) and/or the word "copyright"
- The year of first publication of the work

- The name of the owner of copyright in the work
  Example: © 1994 Jane Doe *or*
  Copyright © 1994 Jane Doe

The notice must be placed on your work in such a manner and location as to "give reasonable notice of the claim of copyright"—for instance, on the first page of a short manuscript or the title page of a book manuscript.

Most magazines and other periodicals or collections are copyrighted; if your work appears in such a publication or collection, it is automatically protected by this blanket copyright notice. If, however, the publication has bought from you only "first rights" (discussed more fully on page 104), *you* remain the copyright owner of the work.

Copyright Registration Procedures

Your work is automatically protected by copyright from the time that it's put onto paper or other physical form, as noted, and actual registration with the Copyright Office is not a *requirement* for protection. There are several advantages to registration, however, and the failure to register your work could, in some instances, be detrimental—particularly if a work becomes commercially valuable, and there is the likelihood of infringement (unauthorized reprint, filming, recording, or other uses). You should register book-length manuscripts, play scripts, and other long works when they're completed but still in manuscript form. It is well worth the $20 registration fee to make sure that there's a public record of your copyright ownership.

These are some of the advantages of registration:

- Registration is ordinarily necessary before any infringement suits may be filed in court.
- If made before or within 5 years of publication, registration will establish evidence in court of the validity of your copyright.
- If registration is made within 3 months after publication of the work or prior to any infringement of it, statutory damages and attorney's fees may be awarded to the copyright owner by the courts. Otherwise, only an award of actual damages and profits is available to the copyright owner.

To register your work, send the following to the Copyright Office, in the same envelope or package:

1. A properly completed application form (obtainable from the Copyright Office)

2. A fee of $20 for each application

3. A deposit (copy) of the work being registered (one copy if the work is unpublished, two if it's published)

All material sent to the Copyright Office should be addressed to the Register of Copyrights, Library of Congress, Washington, DC 20559.

If you write articles, short stories, poems, or other short work, you may be wondering whether it's necessary to register each item separately, and pay a registration fee for each work. Under the most recent revision of the copyright law, you may register on one application—and on payment of a single fee—several individual published works of the same nature (poems, essays, stories). For instance, if you published 20 articles in a single year, you could register them all on one application, for $20. For details on group registration, write to the Copyright Office.

Application forms for registration are supplied free of charge by the Copyright Office, and include the following:

Form TX (for published and unpublished non-dramatic literary works)

Form PA (for published and unpublished works of the performing arts)

Form RE (for claims to renew copyright in works copyrighted under the old law)

Form CA (for supplementary registration to correct or amplify information given in the Copyright Office record of an earlier registration)

Form GR/CP (an adjunct application to be used for registration of a group of contributions to periodicals in addition to an application Form TX or PA)

When writing for forms, state exactly what type of work you wish to copyright, so that you'll receive the proper information for registering that particular work. The effective date of copyright registration is the day on which an acceptable application, deposit, and fee have been received in the Copyright Office. You will receive an official certificate of copyright registration.

How Long Does Copyright Last?

One of the major innovations in the revision of the United States copyright law is that it adopted the basic "life-plus-fifty years" term for copyright protection that's in effect in most other countries. A work created and "fixed in tangible form for the first time" after January 1, 1978, is automatically protected by our copyright law for a term lasting for the author's life, plus an additional 50 years after the author's death. Works created before January 1, 1978, but neither published nor registered for copyright before that date, are now automatically protected by statute for the life of the author plus 50 years.

Rights of Copyright Owners

Copyright owners have the right to reproduce their work;. to prepare derivative works based upon their work; to distribute copies of the work to the public by sale, rental, lease or lending; and to perform or display the work publicly, as in the case of literary, musical, and dramatic works and pantomimes, motion pictures, and other audiovisual works.

As the author of the copyrighted work, you may sell or transfer rights to it in any way or combination that you choose. First rights, for example, would be the only rights usually sold or transferred to a magazine in which your story or article is to be published. Later, you may sell reprint or "second" rights to that story to a second magazine. The permission of the original publisher is not required, although it may be needed for works copyrighted under the previous law. Another example of a transfer: As the author of a published story, you may sell motion-picture rights in that story to a film producer, and you may stipulate that rights are to revert to you if the film is not produced within a specified time.

When a work is written or prepared by an employee within the scope of his or her employment, all rights in such work—called "work for hire"—are the property of the employer, who may register the work in his name or that of the company.

A transfer of ownership may also be requested by a publisher who wishes to buy all rights in your work, but the transfer of all rights is legal only if you agree to such a sale and signify that by signing a written statement or "instrument of conveyance." In the absence of this signed statement, the publisher owns only first rights, or one-time use of the work.

If the work being sold is a book manuscript, make sure your contract, ordinarily drawn up by the publisher and submitted to the author for approval and signature, specifically states the terms of the sale and which rights are included. The style of book contracts is to some extent standardized among publishers, though the language and terms will vary from contract to contract. Among these standardized clauses are the usual guarantees made by both author and publisher. For example, there is ordinarily a clause wherein you, as the author, declare that you are granting the publisher the right to print and publish your book. Other clauses indicate the date on which you will deliver your manuscript in final form to the publisher, that you are responsible for your manuscript (the publisher is not responsible if it's lost or destroyed), and that if the manuscript includes copyrighted work, you will be responsible for obtaining permissions. The publisher also makes certain guarantees, including payment of a specific amount in royalties—generally a certain percentage of the retail price of each copy sold—and times of statements and royalty payments. Other clauses in a contract will be concerned with such matters as the number of free copies given to the author, sale to book clubs, charge for author's corrections, termination of contract in case of bankruptcy, and so forth. The important thing to remember is that if the terms set forth in a contract are not satisfactory to you, the time to take up any question or suggest any change is *before* you sign the contract. The clauses in a book contract are negotiable, to some degree, and you shouldn't be hesitant to discuss possible changes with your editor. If you have an agent, such negotiations are usually conducted by him or her, with your approval.

A final note: Lest you become unduly concerned about this matter of copyright ownership, we would like to emphasize the fact that any reputable publisher endeavors to deal fairly and honestly with an author in all matters relating to the publication of the author's work.

8 | Selected Reference Books

Every writer's personal library should include a comprehensive grammar book, a thesaurus, and an up-to-date dictionary. An unabridged dictionary (which gives every word in the language) is particularly useful, though one of the larger abridgments will ordinarily serve very well. In a good abridgment you will find not only the spelling, definition, and pronunciation of root words, but also some of the prefixes, suffixes, synonyms and antonyms, variations in form, and illustrations of proper usage.

The books in the following list are equally important resources. They are available in most libraries so it isn't necessary to purchase them, but they provide essential information on a variety of subjects. Writers should be aware of them as they prepare their manuscripts for publication, making sure to consult the appropriate text when they have questions.

American Heritage Dictionary of the English Language, Third Edition. Boston: Houghton Mifflin, 1992.

Bartlett, John. *Bartlett's Familiar Quotations, Sixteenth Edition.* Justin Kaplan, General Ed. Boston: Little, Brown, 1992.

Burack, Sylvia K., Ed. *The Writer's Handbook.* Boston: The Writer, Inc.

Chapman, Robert L., Ed. *Roget's International Thesaurus, Fifth Edition.* New York: HarperCollins, 1992.

Chernow, Barbara A., George A. Vallasi, Eds. *The Columbia Encyclopedia, Fifth Edition.* New York: Columbia University Press, 1993.

Chicago Manual of Style. Chicago: University of Chicago Press, Inc., 1993.

Concise Dictionary of American Biography. New York: Scribners, 1964.

Dumond, Val. *Grammar for Grownups.* New York: HarperCollins, 1993.

Fulton, Len, Ed. *The International Directory of Little Magazines and Small Presses.* Paradise, CA: Dustbooks, 1993.

Gordon, Karen Elizabeth. *The New Well-Tempered Sentence: A Punctuation Handbook for the Innocent, the Eager, and the Doomed.* New York: Ticknor & Fields, 1993.

Hart, James D., Ed. *The Oxford Companion to American Literature.* New York: Oxford University Press, 1983.

Harvey, Paul, Sir, Ed. *The Oxford Companion to English Literature.* Oxford: Clarendon Press, 1967.

Home Book of American Quotations. New York: Dodd, Mead, 1967.

Information Please Almanac Atlas & Yearbook. Boston: Houghton Mifflin, 1994.

Literary Market Place. New York: R. R. Bowker, 1993.

National Directory of Magazines. New York: Oxbridge Communications, Inc., 1993.

Ōrrmont, Arthur and Léonie Rosenstiel. *Literary Agents of North America, Fifth Edition.* New York: Author Aid Associates, 1993.

Perkins, George, Barbara Perkins, and Phillip Leininger. *Benét's Reader's Encyclopedia of American Literature.* New York: HarperCollins, 1991.

Reader's Guide to Periodical Literature.

Richards, Gillian and Linda MacColl. *Dramatists Sourcebook.* New York: Theatre Communications Group, 1993.

Ross-Larson, Bruce. *Edit Yourself: A Manual for Everyone Who Works with Words.* New York: Norton, 1982.

Skillin, Marjorie E. *Words into Type, Third Edition.* Englewood Cliffs, NJ: Prentice-Hall, 1986.

Strunk, William, and E. B. White. *The Elements of Style.* New York: Macmillan, 1979.

Urdang, Laurence, Ed. *Dictionary of Confusable Words.* New York: Facts on File, 1988.

Van Doren, Charles, Ed. *Webster's American Biographies.* Springfield, MA: Merriam-Webster, Inc., 1984.

Webster's Dictionary of English Usage. Springfield, MA: Merriam-Webster, Inc., 1989.

Webster's Standard American Style Manual. Springfield, MA: Merriam-Webster, 1985.

INDEX